19.00

Barnes & Noble Critical Studies

General Editor: Anne Smith

The Confidence Man in Modern Fiction

THE CONFIDENCE MAN
IN MODERN FICTION

A Rogue's Gallery with Six Portraits

John G. Blair

BARNES & NOBLE
BOOKS
10 East 53d St., New York 10022
(a division of Harper & Row Publishers, Inc.)

Barnes & Noble Books
Harper & Row, Publishers, Inc.
10 East 53rd Street
New York

ISBN 0–06–490449–0

LC No. 79–50928

First published in the U.S.A. 1979
© 1979 John G. Blair

Printed and bound in Great Britain
MCMLXXIX

Contents

This season, the man of good will will wear his heart up his sleeve, not on it. For better or worse, we who live in this age not only feel but are critically conscious of our emotions. . . . A naïve rhetoric, one that is not confessedly "theatrical" is now impossible in poetry. The honest manly style is today suited only to Iago.

W. H. Auden, 1948

To be is, immutably, to be Iago.

John Fowles, 1966

Acknowledgements

When a book has been long aborning and both its preparation and its subject matter straddle the Atlantic, gratitude for both personal and professional aid accumulates in several countries. Among these many sustainers and supporters I want to thank explicitly colleagues who have read all or part of the manuscript with acuteness and encouragement: Professors George Steiner and Richard Waswo of the University of Geneva and my revered first chairman, Professor Robert Hoopes, now at the University of Massachusetts. An Oakland University Faculty Research Grant gave early impetus and the libraries of the Faculty of Letters in Geneva and Wilson College in Chambersburg, Pennsylvania helped greatly with difficult items. As always my greatest debt is to my family: to my daughter Ann for a model of what sustained and intelligent effort can produce and to my wife Karin. Out of her own work on Camus she has contributed the basic ideas which result in Chapter Five and less tangibly but perhaps more importantly during the years of our introduction to life in Europe, she has proved a stimulating combination of partner and agonist.

Introduction

Lying is a universal human experience. Almost as soon as a child begins mastering language, he or she must also learn that words can lie, can misrepresent, can tell stories. The difficulty of gauging the truthfulness of one's own words or of distinguishing between the trustworthy and the untrustworthy in the assertions of others remains a life-long quandary. Literature itself is a case of licit lying which turns again and again on the uncertain relation between appearance and reality. In times like our own when shared agreements as to what constitutes the "real" are disappearing at an unnerving rate, anyone who claims to speak "truth" is suspect. Under such circumstances a few thoughtful writers may turn to studying the liar in hopes that uncovering the sources and modalities of lying might reveal where we lost track of the true, the good, and the beautiful.

Among all the liars and fabulists in the world the figure of the confidence man towers head and shoulders above the crowd. He convinces you that his riches are fabulous (which of course they are), invites you to join a scheme sure to multiply your own wealth and, as soon as he has your confidence, proves it to be misplaced. If you are a writer—or a reader—no longer sure what view of the world to have confidence in, what notion of right and wrong is trustworthy or how to distinguish the true from the false, what better figure for testing imaginatively your uncertainties. All you need to do is recognize the con man at work and then evaluate his behaviour as it deserves—if you can. Besides, the con man who appears in literature is a generator of fictions for those around him, who himself inhabits a fiction. Hence he simultaneously serves as figure for the writer whose artistic medium must manipulate pretenses and falsehoods even in order to probe the nature of the true and false in the larger world it depicts. In short, the figure of the con man by his very nature stirs up the most troublesome moral, aesthetic, and epistemic uncertainties of our time.

A fairly precise definition of the confidence man as criminal is essential to recognizing the character type in diverse literary settings, even when the criminal prototype is followed from a respectable distance. A police artist's *robot-portrait* of a con man at work reveals that his identifying ploy is to cheat only those who are themselves ready to cheat. He is the swindler raised to the second power, reserving his blandishments for would-be swindlers. An ordinary swindler falsifies legitimate money-making schemes: stocks or bonds, warehouse certificates for vegetable oil, a biography of Howard Hughes or whatever. The victim falls when he naïvely accepts the legitimacy of the bogus scheme. A con man, on the other hand, offers his victim partnership in an illegal scheme, the more sure because it is illicit. The victim must agree in advance to participate in trickery. The popular film *The Sting* (1973) provides a convenient and classic example. After putting up the capital necessary to make a killing, the victim never sees his money or the con man again. At the same time the victim has difficulty complaining to the police because of his own complicity. *The Sting*: "Did you want me to call him for cheating better than I did?"[1] Though the con man's guilt is compounded, the victim is far from innocent, a factor crucial to the moral implications of the figure of the con man.

This criminological definition of my key concept provides a necessary corrective to the laxity of everyday language in which "con man" may be indistinguishable from vague catch-alls like "swindler", "operator", or "wheeler-dealer". When the term is heedlessly extended to related but distinct types like the salesman, the ad man, or the politician, the con man blurs still further into the vague mass of scoundrels, rogues, and rascals who plague our world even as they enliven our literature.

Since the first clear description of a criminal confidence man in English—in Robert Greene's coney-catching pamphlets of 1591— there have appeared occasional works of popular literature which follow the criminal paradigm with precision. Len Deighton's *Only When I Larf* (1968) is a convenient recent example. The direct importation of the criminal type into literature, however, produces nothing more interesting than racy popular fiction. The more rewarding con men studied here want more than mere money for gain. Seeking intangible income like loyalty, faith, or subservience, they allow their authors to probe into the philosophical and moral tenets that undergird Western views of the world. In the process the figure of the confidence man is progressively stretched and extended in significance far beyond his criminal origins.

This study, then, moves away from the criminal prototypes to locate its raw material in works by six important novelists of the last hundred-odd years: from Melville in *The Confidence Man* (1857) to John Fowles in *The Magus* (1966, rev. 1977). While every reader will think of works he might suggest for inclusion, virtually all—on reflection—turn on swindling rather than conning. Think, for example, of Fielding's *Jonathan Wild* (1743), Gogol's *Dead Souls* (1842), or O. Henry's *The Gentle Grafter* (1908), as well as lesser American works like J. J. Hooper's *Some Adventures of Simon Suggs* (1845) or Joe David Brown's *Addie Pray* (1971). Recent works by such writers as Nigel Dennis or John Barth come closer to the mark but would not add significantly to the evolution traced out by the present examples. In short, the works treated here are the major texts exploring the implications of the con man in modern fiction. They are important not because they represent a larger body of works on the same subject but because each pushes further the figure common to them all, a figure who serves as a barometer sensitive to changes in philosophic, moral, and aesthetic presuppositions. Taken separately, each of these novels is memorable literature; taken together, they enlighten each other and literature as an expression of Western civilization in our era.

It should now be clear why this study draws on works from three languages and four national literatures: it is concerned less with comparative literature in a formal sense than with Western literature in a collective sense. My experience as an American living and teaching in Europe for some years convinces me that the West shares not only a common cultural heritage but a common fate as well. In addition, the confidence man as a character type belongs to no single nation as much as to the Western philosophical and religious tradition which insists not only on such world-shaping dichotomies as good and evil, true and false, God and Satan, but also on despising one term in each pair. The con man becomes important in our time precisely because he challenges the easy continuance of such comforting simplicities.

A diachronic perspective is revealing. For Robert Greene and John Milton, a con man was clearly an avatar of the devil. For John Fowles he approaches godhood and only limited irony undercuts this apotheosis. What is revealed step by step through Melville, Gide, Mann, Camus, and Vonnegut is a series of intermediate conceptions which demonstrate a radical inversion in the core values traditional in the West. One by one these settings of the confidence figure demolish familiar presumptions. Melville does away with a world which can make rational "objective" sense. Gide and Mann mock the bourgeois social order built on respectability and social climbing. The three more recent writers focus their attacks on aspects of the moribund Judeo-Christian complex of moral values. Camus lays bare the devastating logic of guilt that undergirds the system. Vonnegut depicts liberal humanitarianism as null and void. Fowles probes the paradoxes of loving kindness: what appears at first to be cruel manipulation of a human being may turn out to be profoundly loving. Not surprisingly these memorable settings of the con man are particularly dense in the last quarter-century. As we approach the present, these novelists are increasingly troubled by just those issues stirred up by the con man as a character type: the uncertain nature of reality and the dubious credibility of traditional morality. These writers, then, both reflect the cultural crises of the West and help to further them.

This study also pursues a complementary synchronic and paradigmatic interest in the con man's way of being in literature. Since a con man can be recognized only through his special relation with his victim, there are constraints on the literary medium in which he can flourish. Only certain settings can accommodate such a figure and only certain treatments of plot and narrative point of view. These six portraits provide a range of literary treatments sufficient to demonstrate the structures appropriate to the character type. For example, the reader can be engaged in the story by way of three basic foci: the author may posit a disengaged observer of the interaction between con man and victim (Melville), or he may allow the con man to tell his own story (Mann), or else have the victim recount his experiences (Fowles). These three primary colourings of narration yield three intermediate possibilities: the con man may be assimilated to the observer (Gide), the observer may merge with the victim (Camus), or the victim may gravitate toward the con man (Vonnegut).

Given the limited range of literary structures appropriate to the confidence figure, these portraits establish a significant evolution. As the con man progressively rises in esteem, the reader's engagement with the figure evolves from detached observation of the encounter between con man and victim into progressively closer identification with the latter. In short, as the con man first sheds his devilish and criminal associations and then approaches deification, we readers find ourselves increasingly subordinate to him.

In addition the evolution of the avatars described here can be projected into a future for the con man in literature which is off the scale established by these portraits. Such a figure requires—and the novels studied here provide—a fictional world sufficiently consistent and shapely that the con man is recognizable by contrast with more conventional and "trustworthy" characters. When "postmodern" fiction abolishes recognizable character and plot, it also passes the outer limits of the con man's visibility in literature. If a fiction is built on the con man's own strategy of shifting appearances, he remains invisible because his habitual protective colouration takes over the background as well as the foreground. If every character acts like a con man, none will be recognizable as such.

In the last few years, as critics have begun to explore the literary implications of the confidence figure, their works suffer from two major defects. Susan Kuhlmann's *Knave, Fool and Genius* (1973) conveniently exemplifies both. Lacking a clear delimitation of the notion "confidence man", she assimilates all sorts of diverse villains. Secondly, she limits herself to one national literature—the American. The United States is important for two basically linguistic reasons: the nineteenth century did produce the term "confidence man" out of the hustle and chicanery of the 1840s[2] and, though the term has long since been imported into England, no precise equivalent exists in the major Continental languages.[3] None the less the examples available in American literature vary

15

excessively from folklore figures to the products of high art such as Melville's.

The remaining recent books locate the confidence man on the periphery of other interests. Richard Boyd Hauck, in *A Cheerful Nihilism* (1971), is primarily concerned with reinterpreting American literature through the concept of the "absurd". The title of Warwick Wadlington's *The Confidence Game in American Literature* (1975) is misleading since he is seriously concerned only with two authors (Melville and Twain) and with a limited sense of "confidence": the varying kinds of faith a reader places in the rhetorical constructs these writers generate.

The present study tries to keep its aims clear and to keep to them. Its tools are essentially those of literary and cultural analysis in whatever terms yield the most appropriate sense in each instance studied. My aim has been to give the lie to those individuals on both sides of the Atlantic who believe that studying con men inevitably becomes a do-it-yourself process. One doesn't have to be one to know one.

NOTES

1. These words are drawn from the sound track of the film, which takes precedence over the later printed adaptation by Robert Weverka (New York, 1974).

2. One of the early appearances of the term, from the *New York Herald* of 8 July 1849, is conveniently reprinted in Hershel Parker's edition of Melville's *The Confidence Man* (New York, 1971), 227.

3. The German *"Hochstapler"* carries a connotation of social climbing or pretension involving imposture. In French most of the possible translations are general catch-alls for swindler or embezzler; thus Melville's novel is translated as *Le grand escroc*. The comparable indicator in Italian is *"truffatore"*, though some dictionaries give *"truffatore alla americana"* as a precise equivalent. Spanish stays on the general plane with *"estafador"*. It would take an extensive but interesting sociolinguistic study to suggest why American English should have developed such relatively fine distinctions between forms of swindling. One might speculate that the United States with a more open and expanding society was more dependent on trust than its European ancestors and hence that it needed more precise labelling for the violations of trust to which it was subject, much as Eskimos need to distinguish more states of snow than do desert dwellers.

1

Parents and Prototypes

> You may perceive it [swindling] to be a prejudicial insinuating
> cozenage; yet is the art of cony-catching so far beyond it in
> subtlety, as the Devil is more honest than the holiest angel.
> —Robert Greene

1. The Criminal

The figure of the confidence man in modern literature owes much
to a distinctive criminal type that has remained substantially un-
changed for centuries. The con man's distinguishing characteristic
lies in the uncommon relationship he maintains with the victim
he exploits. Among all the varied swindlers, rogues, tricksters, and
villains of literature and life, only the confidence man exacts the
moral complicity of his victim as a pre-condition for fleecing him.
To defend himself against a confidence man, all the prospective
victim need do is merely to act honestly. The con man preys only
on those with larceny already in their souls. Hence the criminal
and moral sophistication of the con man: he swindles would-be
swindlers. He is the trickster raised to the second power.

As a model for literary adaptation the criminal prototype maintains a remarkably stable mode of operation. Over at least the
last four centuries his goals and strategies have changed about as
much as the human nature on which he preys. The classic portrait
of the con man at work comes from the pen of Robert Greene,
aided by some unacknowledged borrowing from Gilbert Walker,
who laid bare the con games of the mid-sixteenth century. Greene's
A Notable Discovery of Cozenage (1591) describes rogues and
robbers of several sorts, but his first portrait shows an unmistak-
able "cony-catcher", as such operators were commonly designated
in English till the term "confidence man" emerged from nineteenth-

17

century America. The word "cony" (in Greene's day riming with "money"; by the nineteenth century shifting to "coney" sounded like "bony") echoes the Latin for rabbit, suggesting the simpleton who is all too easily snared by a skilful operator.

Following Greene we must imagine three or more confederates who combine to fleece the victim. They will all be "apparelled like honest civil gentlemen or good fellows, with a smooth face, as if butter would not melt in their mouths."[1] These cony-catchers scan the London crowd looking for a likely mark. They prefer country bumpkins come to town for a session of the courts, but anyone a bit naïve and carrying something in his purse will do. The first step is to establish friendly relations with the victim that can grow into a visit to a tavern where the rabbit is to be skinned.

The con men have an endless variety of means to ingratiate themselves with the victim. In Greene's words:

> The taker-up seemeth a skilful man in all things, who hath by long travail learned without book a thousand policies to insinuate himself into a man's acquaintance. Talk of matters of law, he hath plenty of cases at his fingers' ends, and he hath seen, and tried, and ruled in the King's courts. Speak of grazing and husbandry, no man knoweth more shires than he, nor better which way to raise a gainful commodity, and how the abuses and overtures of prices might be redressed. Finally, enter into what discourse they list, were it into a broom-man's faculty, he knoweth what gains they have for old boots and shoes; yes, and it shall scape him hardly, but that ere your talk break off, he will be your countryman at least, and, peradventure either of kin, ally or some stale sib to you, if your reach far surmount not his.

The number of ploys is endless. If all else fails, the "verser", one of the confederates, once he knows the man's hometown, may stop him on the street pretending to recognize him and ask that he carry a letter home to the parson of his parish. He may even offer some money as an added inducement. Of course the letter is not yet ready, but . . . if we just step into this tavern, it can be written in no time. In short, it would take a teetotaling misanthropic Puritan to insist on being alone in the city in the face of such cunning blandishments.

Once inside the tavern the verser moves to take the cony into his confidence: a friendly game of cards to determine who shall pay for the wine. While a second confederate, the "setter", is away from the table to fulfil some common human need, the verser makes a proposal of apparently innocent fun. The setter and the verser will each name a card at random. After the former shuffles and the latter cuts the cards, they will turn up cards one by one from the bottom of the deck until one or the other card turns up. The person who called that card wins whatever has been bet. The verser proposes that the cony call his card for him. Just to help the fun along, he will cut only a few cards off the top of the deck, and, in the process of setting the large remaining pile on the top of these few, he will give the cony a glimpse of the bottom card. Since there are only those few cards to be turned up before the one the victim has seen, the odds are heavily in favour of that card appearing before the one the setter names at random. Thus, says verser to cony, if you will only call out that bottom card I let you see, we'll have some innocent fun with his fellow —and then, so as not to be mean, we'll let him in on the secret.

Once again it is hard for the cony to refuse. Everything appears so innocent; he won't even handle the cards himself. But in giving his assent to participate in the dishonest game, the cony has made the essential commitment that all criminal con men must secure before they can cheat their victims. The consequences follow rapidly. They play as proposed, and the cony sees how easy it is to win. All is still in fun and the setter is let in on the secret after a few hands. The three are chatting companionably when a third member of the gang bursts in—the "barnacle" in Greene's terminology. Acting rather befuddled with drink, he is invited to sit and share some wine and, of course, to play. Here is a more serious gambler who opposes the verser and his by now confirmed ally, the cony. Enraged at losing several hands in a row, the barnacle may accuse the cony of cheating, forcing further moral compromise on him if he denies it. To recoup his losses, the barnacle raises the stakes, the cony combining funds with the verser to match him. Naturally the cony and verser win most of the time to the further frustration of the barnacle. Finally they are ready for the final plucking of the chicken. The barnacle raises money from the inn-keeper by pawning something; the stakes rise to the limit of the cony's pocket and pawnables; they bet on each card that is turned up. Happily for the cony, as he thinks, the verser makes a very thin cut this time so that the cony's card is bound to come up early. Then they will collect a fabulous haul from the barnacle. The honest odds, after all, are overwhelmingly in their favour. The barnacle, however, has stacked the deck with his card preceding the cony's card.

Suddenly the game is over and the cony has been conned. More than likely he will sorrowfully accept the loss and go his way. With three opponents, he is in no position to try recovering his losses by violence. Even if he suspects he has been cheated, he is in an awkward position to approach a magistrate. Whatever explanation he gives, it must soon become evident that even if he has been cheated, it was in the process of his own attempt to cheat.

Here in Elizabethan dress is the operational mode of the confidence man as criminal. In our own day the game still follows the same essential outlines. The con man and his confederates seek out a well-to-do prospect in a context permitting easy contact between strangers. They establish friendly relations as a means to arousing his curiosity about a money-making scheme, the more sure because it is dishonest. They arrange a "convincer", a trial case where the victim reaps large profits from risking a small amount. If they play their cards right, the victim will eagerly insist on being allowed to join in on the largest scale he can afford. Inevitably some "mischance" occurs between the time when he turns his money over to the con man and the time when the rewards were to have been reaped. The victim is abandoned, stripped of his cash and also any moral basis for complaining to the police. The more prominent he is, the less likely that he will risk having his shenanigans become public knowledge.

The crucial moment comes when the victim is allowed to see what sure and sumptuous gains follow from the dishonesty involved. If he assents at that point, his own greed will likely carry him through to the end. In order to protect himself, all he would have to do is act honestly. Here the con man's essential distinguishing characteristic is evident. Because the victim shares the moral responsibility for wrong-doing, the confidence man can claim, with some more justice than a mere swindler, that he is hardly more dishonest than the conies he victimizes.

For precisely this reason, the confidence man serves well an author interested in probing the moral nature of mankind. Greene, it is true, emphasizes the devilish subtlety of the cony-catchers much more vividly than the corruptibility of their victims. He is not a Puritan but a pamphleteer whose sales might suffer if he stressed the human failings which allow the con men steady success. He knows perfectly well that "men's natures be prone to sin", (140) but he chooses to deemphasize that perspective. In the hands of later writers less concerned with popularity and sales, the moral subtlety implicit in the confidence situation will exert its influence more centrally.

Before we turn directly to the conditions under which the figure of the criminal confidence man emerges in serious literature, a brief portrait of a twentieth-century confidence man at work can demonstrate how little has changed in the criminal's procedure.[2] In twentieth-century America the confidence game has sometimes reached great heights of elaboration: *The Sting* is historically accurate in showing a betting office that can be assembled in an empty store front in a few hours, only to disappear again in case the mark should return the next day. But as one example from the life of "Yellow Kid" Weil shows, the con game never essentially depends on such superstructures. Yellow Kid Weil, who died in 1976 at the impressive age of 100, was surely the most notorious American con man of the first half of this century, working largely out of Chicago. Here is one of his most charming games: Weil, jauntily but not indiscreetly dressed, takes up an expensive box at a local racetrack. He bets only on the last race, when he sends a servant out with a stack of bills in hand. Clearly he has chosen the winner because after the race the servant returns with several stacks of bills. The next day they repeat the performance. By the end of the week several habitués are pressing the genial Weil to reveal his secret. Finally, in confidence, he admits that the last race is fixed and that he gets his signal of how to bet just before the race. Naturally he cannot reveal the means whereby the race is fixed, but on being pressed, he agrees to put some of their money with his for the last race. Sure enough, they all have the winner, as they see when the servant returns with the appropriate winnings for each one. Most of Weil's clients will have risked only a few dollars on this first trial, but with the actual

21

proof of the system in their hands they are likely to drain all bank accounts for a repeat performance the next day. They have had their "convincer". The next day all gather around eagerly. The servant is duly sent out with all the money just before the last race and they settle down to watch, the victims already mentally counting their gains. As the horses near the last turn, Weil jumps from his seat, shouting something to the effect of "Scoundrels, cheats, we've been tricked: I'll kill him!" In a fury, perhaps drawing a pistol, Weil rushes toward the stairs and down them. Later he and the "servant" meet to divide the spoils. Simple and effective, though not to be used again at the same racetrack for some years.

As raw material for literature such con games and their central players are rich in possibilities. Not all the novelists in this study necessarily drew their inspiration directly from criminals of whom they were aware. None the less criminal models can be a direct stimulus to literature. Thomas Mann tells us that his first ideas about Felix Krull came from the memoirs of a Roumanian adventurer named Manolescu.[3] André Gide discusses within *Les Caves du Vatican* an actual Vatican swindle of the early 1890s which is remarkably parallel to the one mounted by Protos in the novel. There is even a chance that Melville was encouraged to investigate confidence men by an imposter who successfully passed himself off as a young author named Herman Melville.[4] Suffice it to say that the steady availability of criminal con men in our world and their essentially identical techniques over a long period guarantees the constant possibility of inspiration for literature.

2. The Picaresque Rogue

As a figure in modern literature, the confidence man derives not simply from criminal prototypes, but also from the literary tradition of the picaresque. In the process of sorting out the ways in which the confidence man diverges from both models, we can see more clearly the distinctive literary modalities that impinge on the works central to this study.

The ancestry of the picaresque rogue extends back to mythological precedents. Hermes in Greek and Odin/Loki in Norse mythology prefigure the easy-going trickster who gets away with whatever he can.[5] The more immediate precedents in the Renaissance begin in Spanish with *Lazarillo de Tormes* (1554) with some help, perhaps, from such folk figures as Till Eulenspiegel. Through to its flowering in eighteenth-century France and England, the genre of the picaresque retains reasonably stable characteristics.

The central figure, the picaresque rogue, is normally an outsider in relation to his social setting. Whether by necessity or high spirits, he lives by his wits, manipulating those around him by simulating the accepted values of the society through which he moves. As Alastair Fowler puts it, he is always "taking credit" for something he is not.[6] He is a man of the world devoted to advancing his own interests by any available means. Thus he is typically an amoral scamp who delights in exploiting every new turn of events with quick intelligence.

The rogue invites a reader's holiday from serious moral or intellectual reflection. The reader is encouraged to identify with the rogue and his easy adventurous spirit, to delight in his successes more than to condemn his excesses of improper behaviour. In the words of Claudio Guillen, author of the most important recent description of the *picaro*, he soon learns that there is no material survival outside of society, and no real refuge—no pastoral paradise—beyond it. Social role-playing is as ludicrous as it is indispensible.[7] The confidence man, by contrast, has usually lost his sense of the ludicrous. Game-playing becomes a loaded activity which is the source of his being. Hence such figures commonly evoke a moral seriousness rare among picaresque rogues. Thus Robert Greene, as we have seen, treats his con men not as scamps but as manifestations of the devil.

The different degrees of moral seriousness typically surrounding these two types helps also to differentiate the apparently similar literary environments the two usually inhabit. Both the *picaro* and the con man are most at home in an episodic plot set largely in public places where strangers can mix easily. The *picaro* requires such a plot and setting because, as Robert Heilman puts it in his brief anatomy of the genre, he is deliberately a shallow character, the figure for saucy fun. "Instead of depth and rigour we have speed and multiplicity: since without 'character' a story cannot indefinitely be spun out of one set of circumstances, one situation must soon be replaced by another; and since living by

23

wits alone is not conducive to lone residence, one scene normally gives way to another without much delay."[8] The confidence man also invites an episodic plot and lacks "character", but for quite different reasons.

The confidence man has no personal "character" because a stable "self" would be incompatible with his calling. Such a character is an extreme among human types devoted to dissimulation. It is difficult if not impossible to depict him apart from the succession of roles he adopts for his victims. Insofar as he acquires a personality or an individual identity, he ceases to be a confidence man and becomes another ordinary mortal, struggling with the relation between his inner and outer selves. The distinctive nature of the con man as character is that he is absorbed into the illusions he creates for those around him. The rogue may be shallow, but the con man is essentially without a self.

Hence the confidence man belongs in an episodic plot because he possesses no ground of continuity on the basis of which to perpetuate "himself". He has no more stability than an actor who is seen only in an endless series of roles. The con man may briefly leave the stage, but he can never leave the theatre to take up a private and extraprofessional life. He has no personal identity and, in the long run, no psychology. In literature he is usually presented from the outside; strictly speaking, he has no inside.

A story centered around a con man must share his impermanence. As a criminal he requires a convenient means to avoid detection and capture. The racetrack stunt of Yellow Kid Weil is too risky to try again in the same spot. Successive settings guaranteeing anonymity are necessary. Thus Felix Krull takes off on a world tour impersonating a nobleman from Luxembourg; the relatives he is to meet will not have seen him since early childhood if at all. Otherwise, if a con man remains in one location as does Camus's Jean-Baptiste Clamence, his surroundings must be conducive to the coming and going of his customers. The shifting incidents that make up the narrative serve also to signal the reader that a confidence man is at work. Once we see him adopting different masks for different scenes we can more surely recognize him for what he is.

The family background of the confidence character usually remains vague. Any life arrangements that presume continuity of self or circumstances are impossible for him. Literature often dramatizes his nature by assigning him obscure parentage, or by making him a homeless wanderer like Kurt Vonnegut's Bokonon. The same, of course, is often true of the rogue, though for different reasons. The author of a picaresque tale may hide the hero's parentage for a time to justify his wandering about and often enough to set up a neat and satisfying ending when the hero safely re-enters the Establishment. The con man, on the other hand, can never have a clear social or personal identity. For him, identity, excitement, even existence itself are tied to his professional life. Thus we see Melville's man in a grey suit languishing during the temporary absence of any prospects:

> If a drunkard in a sober fit is the dullest of mortals, an enthusiast in a reason-fit is not the most lively. And this, without prejudice to his greatly improved understanding; for, if his elation was the height of his madness, his despondency is but the extreme of his sanity. Something thus now, to all appearance, with the man in grey. Society his stimulus, loneliness was his lethargy. Loneliness, like the sea-breeze, blowing off from a thousand leagues of blankness, he did not find, as veteran solitaires do, if anything, too bracing. In short, left to himself, with none to charm forth his latent lymphatic, he insensibly resumes his original air, a quiescent one, blended of sad humility and demureness.[9]

Through Melville's lumbering humour emerges the portrait of a con man without a client subsiding like a balloon with a slow leak. Solitude being unnatural and uncomfortable for him, the man in grey soon heads off to accost someone who can "charm forth his latent lymphatic". The activity of the game is what animates him.

This penchant for the game itself helps to define the different motive forces behind the superficially similar episodic plots which carry the confidence man and the picaresque rogue along their separate ways. The rogue is usually pushed on from one adventure to the next by some external event, a storm or the need to avoid paying a bill. Each new circumstance challenges his powers of invention and adaptation. The con man, on the other hand, once he has brought any given client to the climax of the game, must by the logic of his character seek out still another prospect.

25

For both the rogue and the con man the episodic plot encourages apposite settings. Anonymity is the medium in which the confidence man flourishes. He is unimaginable in a stable rural society where everyone knows everyone else. At the very least he needs a county fair or a travelling show. Still better is a large city or a means of public transportation where everyone present is a stranger: a train as in *The Sting* or the Mississippi River steamer which Melville exploits. In such surroundings each man's past remains unverifiable and consequently malleable. The picaresque rogue inhabits a similar literary world of public houses or stage coaches, but rarely exploits the circumstances with the seriousness of the confidence man. The confidence man seeks not consent to the rules of an essentially innocent game, but collusion in transgressing the legal and moral order.

If the confidence man differs from the rogue in the criminal seriousness of the issues at stake, that does not imply that all literary settings of the confidence man share the same level of seriousness. There are two broadly different literary traditions depicting confidence men, only one of which is centrally important for this study. There is a long tradition of popular criminal literature, beginning with Robert Greene himself, which aims primarily at sensationalism or entertainment or both. This tradition extends through such works in English as Henry Fielding's *Jonathan Wild* (1743), Johnson Hooper's *Simon Suggs* (1845) and O. Henry's *The Gentle Grafter* (1908). A good recent example is Len Deighton's *Only When I Larf* (1968). Insofar as they have a serious purpose, most such works aim at alarming the reader about the state of society. They serve primarily as entertainment in the sense that they presume an agreed-upon set of values shared by the writer and his audience, the values of good sense or reform as the case may be. The elusive questions implicit in the obscure nature of the confidence man are left aside.

The other literary approach to the confidence man is the subject of this book. In the hands of these writers the con man becomes a means of probing the nature of man and his world. In particular they use the con man as a vehicle for exploring and testing moral and intellectual values. Because the confidence man seems illusory himself, swallowed up in the fabrications he offers the world, he challenges easy definitions of what is real. Because his fabrications seem reprehensible yet may sometimes, as in John Fowles' *The Magus*, seem to produce positive results for human kind, he challenges traditional notions of right and wrong.

The reader, for whose sake the literature exists, is inescapably concerned with his own certainties. His moral and philosophic presuppositions, ultimately his soul, are at stake in the encounter. Where the rogue is motivated by adventure and the simple criminal by money, the sophisticated confidence man in modern literature seeks something much more valuable. As Melville's one-legged man puts it: "You two green-horns! Money, you think, is the sole motive to pains and hazard, deception and deviltry, in this world. How much money did the devil make by gulling Eve?" (36). In John Milton's portrait of a confidence man at work gulling Eve we find a memorable statement of the traditional Western certainties, moral and intellectual, which are essential to define the context in which major writers of more recent time have approached the figure of the confidence man.

3. The Miltonic Devil

John Milton knew a devil when he saw one. He could set out, in *Paradise Lost*, to justify God's ways to men because he felt confident of his understanding of the nature of God and His creation. As one of the last great spokesmen for a long Christian and humanist tradition stretching back through the Renaissance and the Middle Ages even to the classical Greeks, Milton had available to him certainties which allowed the clear recognition and condemnation of deviltry. The search to replace those fading certainties is one of the essential stimuli for later writers to explore the figure of the confidence man.

Milton's portrait of a con man at work occurs in Book IX of *Paradise Lost* in the person of Satan enticing Eve to eat the fatal fruit. Unlike Robert Greene, Milton was not trying to expose the criminal type and his techniques but rather seeking the most effective means to dramatize the Devil at work to subvert mankind. The result is a confidence man.

Satan, it is true, begins his seduction less malignly. His initial ploys are more suited to the lesser figure of the advertising man. He first merchandises a social self-consciousness comparable to

27

the status-consciousness that both gives rise to and is reinforced by modern sales techniques. In effect numbers are substituted for qualities so that Eve, if she accepts his flattery, will begin to measure her beauty in terms of the number and sophistication of her admirers:

> ... but here
> In this enclosure wild, these beasts among,
> Beholders rude, and shallow to discern
> Half what in thee is fair, one man except,
> Who sees thee? (and what is one?) who shouldst be seen
> A Goddess among Gods, adored and served
> By angels numberless, thy daily train.
>
> (11. 542–48)

What good is consumption if it isn't conspicuous?

Eve responds with frank curiosity about how a serpent could come to rise above his station to achieve human speech, and Satan's reply, describing his sampling of the forbidden fruit, offers a veritable handbook of techniques for modern publicity.

> To satisfy the sharp desire I had
> Of tasting those fair apples, I resolved
> Not to defer; hunger and thirst at once,
> Powerful persuaders, quickened at the scent
> Of that alluring fruit, urged me so keen.
> About that mossy trunk I wound me soon,
> For high from ground the branches would require
> Thy utmost reach or Adam's:

"Just picture yourself already there."

> round the tree
> All other beasts that saw, with like desire
> Longing and envying stood, but could not reach.

"Everybody wants one."

> Amid the tree now got, where plenty hung
> Tempting so nigh, to pluck and eat my fill
> I spared not, for such pleasure till that hour
> At feed or fountain never had I found.
>
> (11. 584–97)

"Unbeatable flavour."

Thus far Satan has effectively involved Eve's ego by such advertising ploys. He is now ready, once they have reached the forbidden tree, to increase the seriousness of the game. A mere swindler could have plucked an apple and brought it to Eve, claiming that it was an ordinary fruit, but then her own moral responsibility would not have been engaged. Mere trickery cannot bring about the Fall. Satan must, like the confidence man, entice her to seek an illegitimate gain so that she herself accomplishes the act. He presents her with the necessary "convincer":

> ... look on me,
> Me who have touched and tasted, yet both live,
> And life more perfect have attained than fate
> Meant me, by venturing higher than my lot.
>   (11. 687–90)

Then there remains only to elaborate the tantalizing prospect of the gain to be hers at the small price of disobedience.

> ... in the day
> Ye eat thereof, your eyes that seem so clear,
> Yet are but dim, shall perfectly be then
> Opened and cleared, and yet shall be as Gods,
> Knowing both good and evil as they know.
> That ye should be as Gods, since I as man,
> Internal Man, is but proportion meet,
> I of brute human, ye of human Gods.
>   (11. 705–712)

Eve, of course, accepts the confidence gambit, and the Fall rocks all creation.

The reasons why Milton chose to make Satan in the Garden act as a confidence man go beyond his need to involve Eve's direct moral responsibility for the Fall. In the Garden before the Fall, all creatures are themselves; they lack the self-consciousness necessary to dissembling. By way of contrast, Satan, already fallen, appears as a confidence man, the most sophisticated of duplicitous and hypocritical beings. The tree Eve and Adam eat of is, after all, the Tree of the Knowledge of Good and Evil. With their eating come not simply lust and bodily shame, but also the conscious awareness of the difference between the inner self and the outer presentation of self. Willful falsification immediately becomes

29

possible: Eve can consider dissembling for Adam, thereby perpetuating the evil manipulations practised on her by Satan:

> But to Adam in what sort
> Shall I appear? Shall I to him make known
> As yet my change, and give him to partake
> Full happiness with me, or rather not,
> But keep the odds of knowledge in my power
> Without copartner? so to add what wants
> In female sex, the more to draw his love,
> And render me more equal, and perhaps,
> A thing not undesirable, sometime
> Superior; for inferior who is free?
>
> (11. 816–825)

Eve abandons this option, but only after demonstrating that she herself is now capable of understanding and even performing confidence tricks.

For Milton there is no ambiguity in the nature of the Devil and when Satan acts to subvert mankind, he naturally assumes the techniques of the confidence man. Milton has no uncertainties because both recognition and condemnation of the Devil emerge from the nature of the world understood by "right reason". Milton accepted no distinction between intellectual and moral knowledge. Both were subsumed in the overarching Truth whose name was God. In effect, since everything in existence was created by the Godhead, everything in its own unfallen nature participates in the goodness and rightness of the creating Truth. Right reason, for men, implies not abstract or discursive reasoning but man's active taking of his appointed place in the creation. It implies awareness of his proper nature and the simultaneous will to fulfil it in action. In the words of Robert Hoopes:

> The function of the human mind as a whole is to know; the function of the faculty of reason or judgement is to discriminate between true and false things *to be done*, or between right and wrong. Reason thus simultaneously disposed, so that it presides with equal validity and certainty over the realms of intellect and morality, is what is meant by "right reason". Such a view maintains, in other words, that reason is not just "a subjective faculty of the mind"; it is instead "a principle inherent in reality".[10]

30

The difficulty of Milton's concept for twentieth-century minds lies at least partly in their tendency to conceive reason as a distinct faculty of mind subject to its own shaping forms and rules. Reason no longer seems conterminous with "objective reality". For Milton both the human knower and the creatures he knows are linked by their common origin in the Creator. Even after the Fall a man may, with the help of Grace, become aware of the proper order of creation and his place within it. And awareness implies simultaneous action in the creation to fulfil his place and nature. For Milton man is not doomed to act as a confidence man; that is the province of the insistently unregenerate, the Devil himself.

Milton, of course, was not simply expressing his own convictions, but giving memorable expression to a long-standing Christian and humanist tradition. That same tradition allowed Robert Greene an easy identification of his cony-catchers with the Devil. He knew as well as Milton that the Devil could at will appear more honest than the holiest angel. But because he was more pamphleteer than moralist, Greene tended to place all the blame on the confidence man for subverting naïve mortals. Milton places the blame where it belongs, on the victim as well as the con man. Only those who respond with larceny in their hearts can fall victim to a confidence scheme.

Milton's is the last great statement that clearly identifies the confidence man and the Devil. For the writers who form the main body of this study, intellectual knowledge has at best a tenuous connection with moral knowledge, and either recognition of the confidence man or judgment of him (or both) seems problematical. Lacking Milton's certainties, these writers were obliged to search out and articulate a personal vision of the moral and intellectual universe. That they chose to centre these works around the figure of the confidence man indicates their distrust of conventional approaches to morality and their uncertainty about the real shape of the world. The confidence man as perpetual shapeshifter could become a vehicle for dramatizing a writer's own uncertain and shifting notions of what was true and right. This is especially so for Herman Melville, author of the first major setting of the confidence man in modern fiction.

31

NOTES

1. Because of the relative scarcity of the original edition and the 1924 Bodley Head Quarto of Greene's pamphlet, I quote from the best edition now in print: *The Elizabethan Underworld,* ed. A. V. Judges (London, 1930, 1965), 123. Page references to this edition appear in parentheses within my text. Judges also conveniently reprints Gilbert Walker's *A Manifest Detection of Dice-play* (1552), which was the source of several closely paraphrased passages in Greene, including the one about the "taker-up" quoted in the text.

2. The best study of modern American con men is David Maurer, *The Big Con* (Indianapolis, 1940), from which this example is drawn. Also interesting is *"Yellow Kid" Weil: Con Man,* his autobiography (New York, 1948). A police textbook giving careful coverage to the varieties of the con game is John C. R. MacDonald, *Crime is a Business: Buncos, Rackets, Confidence Schemes* (Palo Alto, 1939).

3. Manolescu, whose real name was Furst Lahovary, published his *Memoiren* (Berlin, 1908), the same year he died. *Le Figaro,* shortly after his death at 37 on 9 January of that year, recalled his self-ordained title as "le Roi des escrocs d'hôtel". For Mann's remark see "Preface" to *Stories of Three Decades,* trans. H. T. Lowe-Porter (New York, 1936), vii.

4. Jay Leyda presumes Melville's knowledge of the imposter "Herman Melville" who worked the South in 1850 selling orders for "his" books —cash in advance. See the *Melville Log* (New York, 1951), xxx and 377–78. Additional speculative evidence appears in Paschal Reeves, "The Deaf-Mute in *The Confidence Man*: Melville's Imposter in Action", *Modern Language Notes,* 75 (January 1960), 18–20.

5. The complex interrelation of rhetoric, commerce, travel, lying, and profit in early Greek culture is the subject of Norman O. Brown's interesting study *Hermes the Thief* (Madison, Wisconsin, 1947 and New York, 1969). For a careful study of the relevant figures in Norse mythology see E. O. G. Turville-Petre, *Myth and Religion of the North* (London, 1964).

6. See "The Confidence Man", *The Listener* (4 May 1961), 781, 984.

7. "Toward a Definition of the Picaresque", in *Literature as System* (1971), 80.

8. "Variations on Picaresque (Felix Krull)" as reprinted in *Thomas Mann, A Collection of Critical Essays,* ed. Henry Hatfield (Englewood Cliffs, N.J., 1964), 136–37.

9. For all quotations from Melville's novel I use Elizabeth Foster's edition of *The Confidence-Man: His Masquerade* (New York, 1954), here page 48. All succeeding quotations are indicated by page numbers in parentheses within the text.

10. *Right Reason in the English Renaissance* (Cambridge, Mass., 1967), 4, italics in original.

2

Herman Melville and God as a Con Man

> Doubts, may be . . . but not knowledge; for how, by examin-
> ing the book, should I think I knew any more than I now think
> I do; since, if it be the true book, I think so already; and since
> if it be otherwise, then I have never seen the true one, and don't
> know what that ought to look like.
> —Melville, *The Confidence-Man*

John Milton needed no term for "confidence man". The felt
reality of Christianity, sustained and confirmed by a trust-inspired
tradition, dictated that the Devil's bag of tricks would include
those used by confidence men whether labelled as such or not.
Melville, writing nearly two centuries later, would have to start
from the opposite position. He had the term, an American neo-
logism which had appeared in the preceding decade, but instead
of a faith he lived with profound uncertainties about the nature of
this world and the next. The resulting fiction, first published in
1857, is the first portrait of the con man in modern fiction, one
that remains the most far-reaching of all in many respects.

If a confidence man offers appearances whose reality is equivocal, so does fiction and so does the universe as Melville
conceived it by the mid-1850s. Hence his novel presents multi-
layered appearances which confound the reader with multiple
hints, implications, and grounds for suspicion. But all the while
the text never supplies evidence sufficient to determine just who is
doing what to whom. If a reader should leap to define a reality
behind these elaborated appearances, he does so on the basis of
a personal faith (confidence) which he imports into Melville's text.
He will have missed many of Melville's nuances, but he will none

the less have acted out the text's implication that "realities" can only be perceived on the basis of one's confidence in them.

The critic's job of work in the face of such a radically ambiguous and elusive text is to proceed cautiously in order to lay bare the author's strategy. The easiest entry is through the limited access to "events" that Melville allows his reader. The reader is tied neither to the putative confidence men nor to their apparent victims. Instead an ostensibly disengaged narrator reports what happens. This narrator, then, controls whatever aspects of the confidence situation will be relevant here. Partly these are moral. The narrator hints at connections between the apparent confidence men and the devil as if to imply that there would be no problem in condemning their activities if only one could be sure that they indeed are confidence men. But the problem of knowledge is prior and fundamental. The novel never provides grounds for sufficient confidence in any particular interpretation of events and hence judgment rests in suspension.

This elusive narrator is admirably resourceful in his ability to transmit events and characters without interpreting them. He achieves his end largely through studied stylistic devices but also through careful exploitation of setting and the uncertainty implicit in metaphor. These latter two devices begin working in the first two chapters which constitute a convenient microcosm for the whole. First the setting. A Mississippi River steamboat, the *Fidèle* no less, is an ideal setting for confidence men to work. The reader takes additional warning of possible shenanigans when the day of the journey is announced as April Fool's Day. All the passengers are strangers and each stranger knows of another only what the latter chooses to present him, in dress or words or actions, about his status in the world or his past. The narrator will even hint of the presence of confidence men on board this ship of fools:

> As among Chaucer's Canterbury pilgrims, or those oriental ones crossing the Red Sea towards Mecca in the festival month, there was no lack of variety. Natives of all sorts, and foreigners; men of business and men of pleasure; parlour men and backwoodsmen; farm-hunters and fame-hunters; heiress-hunters, gold-hunters, buffalo-hunters; bee-hunters, happiness-hunters, truth-hunters, and still keener hunters after all these hunters.

(8)

The last named are perhaps con men, some eight to ten suspicious
characters that continually accost their fellows asking for something or other.[1] But having set the scene and hinted at their
presence, the narrator will offer nothing more determinate than
further grounds for suspicion.

If the setting is suggestive, so is the narrator's handling of the
first scene. Into this microcosm of "that multiform pilgrim species,
man" (8) comes a deaf-mute, who arrives at dawn as suddenly as
a sun-god from a distant Peruvian tradition. Whether we are to
take him as a sun-god or not remains obscure because the narrator
does no more than drop the simile in our laps. If the comparison
implies a similarity, it also implies a distinction. The reader is
no more clearly informed than before.[2]

The narrator continues his discreet evasiveness by simply reporting events without characterizing them. On one side the deaf-
mute tries to attract the crowd's attention to his quotations from
I Corinthians xiii on the trusting nature of charity. On the other
side the ship's barber hangs out his habitual sign refusing credit:
"No Trust." The extremes are in view and the reader is left to
make of them what he can. To dramatize the point the narrator
in Chapter Two, "Showing That Many Men Have Many Minds",
reports in short phrases what nineteen different anonymous characters think of the lamb-like deaf-mute. He seems anything from
saint to sinner, from innocent to rascal, depending on the pre-
judgments of those who view him. The narrator notes that these
characters had not witnessed the events of Chapter One and hence
had no evidence at all on which to base their projections. The
narrator, in short, is not above a parable so long as it reinforces
the indeterminacy of the story he is recounting.

The narrator's stylistic strategy is comparably non-assertive.
From time to time he poses as omniscient in the sense that he can
report thoughts and offer interpretations of a motivation. But
whenever he does, he so qualifies his judgement with "perhaps"
"it may be", or similar disclaimers of certainty that the reader is
once again left responsible for his own interpretation. R. W. B.
Lewis rightly labels such prose as "self-erasing".[3] A single example
must suffice, the introduction of one Charlie Noble:

> But, on the whole, it could not be fairly said that his appearance
> was unprepossessing; indeed, to the congenial, it would have been

35

doubtless not uncongenial; while to others, it would not fail to be at least curiously interesting, from the warm air of florid cordiality, contrasting itself with one knows not what kind of aguish sallowness of saving discretion lurking behind it. Ungracious critics might have thought that the manner flushed the man, something in the same fictitious way that the vest flushed the cheek. (158–59)

Such baroquely periodic sentences, filled with double negatives and indirect qualifications, may be associated historically with careful and precise formulation of ideas, but here they specifically blur communication. Most readers will presumably sense unwholesomeness in Charlie Noble thus presented, but strictly speaking, the narrator has asserted nothing. He has merely reported what first impressions would strike two observers with opposite predilections. The reader must himself side with either the congenial observers or the ungracious critics of Charlie Noble. Once again the essential problem of the novel, this time in stylistic microcosm.

The genius and difficulty of Melville's work is that he continues throughout to maintain such radical ambiguity. The reader can only identify confidence men at work insofar as he chooses to distrust smooth-talking strangers who appeal to the confidence of those around him. Such a reader can find confirmation for his identification only by treating the equivocal text as a self-reflecting mirror. Indeed numerous critics have done so for decades.[4]

Melville's interest, however, is more rigorously philosophical. Before one can recognize con men at work, certain epistemic presumptions must be made. Melville affirms that neither reader nor character can determine the presence of con men except on the basis of some commitment of confidence on his own part.[5] Hence Melville explores all the possible ramifications of the notion "confidence". Through his radically disjoint and episodic plot, Melville again and again juxtaposes characters who are either distrustful on principle or else proponents of easy confidence in whatever appearances are presented them. In each of the three main groups of encounters (between men who appeal to confidence and those who are solicited) we find at least one representative of each extreme position plus a variety of intermediate possibilities. Thus in the first group we find a one-legged cynic who distrusts everything matched against a good-hearted Methodist minister who equates charitable trust and Christian faith. Each acts on the basis of his own predilections, but the narrator refuses to certify which, if either, is justified in his views.[6] Thus the reader finds his own uncertainties dramatized on the level of the characters who must commit themselves beyond the available evidence to one position of confidence or another.

The three main groups of encounters involving possible con men and putative victims divide the text into three sections with increasingly serious philosophical overtones. The first group turns largely on requests for funds, "charity", put to "fortunate" characters on behalf of others who appear less well off than they. Thus in Chapters III through XIII we witness four possible con men soliciting a number of potential benefactors. Considerable simplification is inescapable because of the proliferation of characters and incidents, but we can at least examine a typical case or two.

Possible Con Men	Chief Clients
Black Guinea	Episcopal Clergyman
Man with a Weed	Good-hearted Merchant
(John Ringman)	(Henry Roberts)
Man in a Grey Suit	Sophomoric Collegian
Man in Travelling Cap (Stock-	Gentleman with Gold
Transfer Agent, later	Sleeve Buttons
identified as Mr. Truman)	Charitable Lady

Perhaps because they are relatively prosperous themselves, these clients assent with relative ease to the solicitations of the putative con men. The naïve collegian rejects the philosophical man with a weed as too glum but happily invests money with the stock-transfer agent who makes him feel part of a bluff, hearty, masculine world. Still more startling is the man in gold sleeve buttons who wears white gloves so as not to dirty his hands. He listens somewhat incredulously as the man in grey describes his project for a World Charity operated on Wall-Street principles: "For doing good to the world once for all and having done with it" (46). The man with gold sleeve buttons, despite his having sufficient worldly wisdom to recognize the absurdity of the scheme and the possibility of deception, contributes none the less because the truth of the matter is less to him than his flattering self-image as the most generous of men.

All the clients of this group already subscribe to a map of the moral world, a hierarchy of values in which they place their confidence and establish their identities. Hence they contribute money above all to confirm their standing in terms of their personal orthodoxies. They demonstrate the sincerity of their beliefs by putting their money where their mouths are.

This positive and trusting chorus is broken by Henry Roberts, the good-hearted merchant, who has already contributed generously to the unfortunate man with a weed and invested on his advice in the Black Rapids Coal Company. At the end of Chapter XIII, inspired by a friendly glass of champagne shared with the stock-transfer agent, he bursts out even to his own surprise: " 'Ah, wine is good, and confidence is good; but can wine or confidence percolate down through all the stony strata of hard considerations and drop warmly and ruddily into the cold cave of truth? Truth will *not* be comforted.' " (74, italics in original.) This sobering perspective not only elicits the narrator's literary and epistemic theorizing in Chapter XIV (to be treated later) but prefigures the more serious tone of the second set of encounters between possible con men and their apparent victims. In the meantime this first group of encounters has not helped the reader with *his* problem of knowledge because he can be no more sure than the contributors about the legitimacy of the demands for charity. There are multiple grounds for suspicion but no decisive evidence emerges.

The second series of encounters (Chapters XVI–XXIII) seems more serious primarily because the possible con men approach characters who are themselves unfortunate. Through personal suffering they have lost the naïve confidence that they know the shape of the moral or the physical universe and hence they are suspicious of remedies offered to ease their present pain. They are less confident in all senses of the word, though they would be happy to find something worthy of their confidence. Instead of charity, the root issue is hope. Because these clients press their accosters more closely about the grounds on which they ask for trust, these encounters are substantially longer than in the first group. There is time to deal only with the most interesting, starting with the sick man.

Possible Con Men	*Chief Clients*
Man in Travelling Cap	Old Miser
(Mr. Truman)	Sick Man
Herb-Doctor	Soldier of Fortune
Philosophical Intelligence	Pitch, the Missouri Farmer
Officer	

Chapter XVI, like a number of others, bears a significantly punning title: "A Sick Man, After Some Impatience, Is Induced to Become a Patient." The pun, as I have shown elsewhere,[7] is one of Melville's devices for circularity which defeats the reader's desire to resolve the essential ambiguities. In this case it defeats the patient as well. He has been "impatient" in the double sense of refusing the Herb-Doctor's Omni-Balsamic Reinvigorator, hence not becoming his patient, yet at the same time he has been impatient to find some remedy for his ills. The Herb-Doctor offers the patient hope in direct proportional exchange for whatever confidence the latter places in the remedy. But the patient must be very patient indeed, assigning no limits to the time he is willing to wait for results. A cure can be hoped for "not in a day, nor a week, nor perhaps a month, but sooner or later" (92).

Also the patient must swallow a good deal of shoddy logic along with his pills. He is invited to trust the herbs for the backhanded reason that one cannot be cured by them if he has no confidence in their efficacy. Psychosomatic medicine provides some evidence to support this proposition, but all that really concerns the patient seeking health is the unjustified converse—that having confidence in the remedy will produce a cure. Thus the sick man is thrust back on his willingness to trust. Having exhausted all other medical means he knows of, he has little choice but to accept. No confidence, no possibility of cure. The Herb-Doctor thereupon undercuts even this reluctant faith by warning the patient of possible imitations of his remedy. He offers a vacuous test for the legitimacy of replacement bottles which covertly satirizes the Pauline Christianity from which it is adopted. "Prove all the vials; trust those which are true." (93, I Thessalonians v: 21). The test is hollow because the patient must wait patiently, forever if necessary, for the medicine to work. No wonder the hopeless sick man laments: "But to doubt, to suspect, to prove—

to have all this wearing work to be doing continually—how opposed to confidence. It is evil" (93).

If the patient makes little progress with his problem of confidence, shouldn't at least the reader be sure, for once, that the Herb-Doctor is a charlatan, a quack, and hence, broadly speaking, a confidence man? Not conclusively, any more than one could condemn St. Paul, whose test for legitimacy the Herb-Doctor borrows. To be sure, the appearances are generally for St. Paul and against the Herb-Doctor, but all the bad logic and unconsoling consolations in the world could not prove that his remedy will not work, the only grounds on which we could certainly identify him as a charlatan. One suspects Melville of setting the episode up just to bait us with the complexities of confidence and to tempt us once again to go beyond the evidence by committing our own confidence.

This second group concludes with the one character who has traditionally been viewed as having penetrated the ruses going on around him: Pitch, the Missouri farmer.[8] Pitch fends off the Herb-Doctor only to place his confidence momentarily in the PIO man (from the Philosophical Intelligence Office). Pitch is travelling to find a machine to take over part of his farm work after a succession of thirty-five unsatisfactory boys. The PIO man claims to represent an employment agency which promises to locate a good farm boy on the basis of a "scientific" study of boyhood. Being a good rationalist, Pitch commits his trust to "science", which he presumes to mean the careful derivation of conclusions from experience. Shortly after Pitch pays for a boy, an ominous bluff near Cairo, Illinois, called "The Devil's Joke" (Melville's invention) suggests to him that the "science" involved was nothing more than the justification of desired conclusions on the basis of analogy.

Pitch is the only character to conclude independently that he has been duped. The fever-invested swamps around Cairo prompt thoughts of irradicable evil in the world and suddenly all the PIO man's analogies seem false. Note however that Melville's narrator does not allow certain confirmation that Pitch's reversed judgement is accurate. When Pitch associates the PIO man with a snake, perhaps *the* snake, the narrator keeps all in question by pointing out that this conclusion is itself only another analogy:

40

"The doctrine of analogies recurs. Fallacious enough doctrine when wielded against one's prejudices, but in corroboration of cherished suspicions not without likelihood" (148). The coziness of the final "not without likelihood" suggests that the narrator and Melville behind him know perfectly well what they are doing—tossing the ball back into the reader's lap.

With his reinforced distrust of mankind, Pitch signals the more intense character of the third group of encounters in Chapters XXIV–XLIII. Here individuals who are committed in varying degrees to distrust encounter a master advocate of confidence raised now to a quasi-religious principle. Charity and hope are succeeded by faith as the essential issue.

Advocate of Confidence	Chief Distrusters
The Cosmopolitan	Pitch (again)
(Frank Goodman)	Charlie Noble
	Mark Winsome
	Egbert, Winsome's practical disciple
	Ship's Barber (William Cream)

The cosmopolitan can take on such a varied crowd because he is a world traveller with a global view of the intricacies of human trust. His fantastic parti-coloured robe joins bits of national costumes from around the world and his philosophy pretends to similar transcendence of parochial boundaries. He aims at nothing less than elevating confidence into a new religion called Geniality. The genial view dictates easy-going camaraderie, confirmed by shared wine, tobacco, and "friendly loans". As the cosmopolitan confirms to Pitch: "Life is a pic-nic en costume; one must take a part, assume a character, stand ready in a sensible way to play the fool" (152). When good fellowship reigns supreme, unpleasant possibilities are rejected out of hand as too horrible to be true. Negative judgments, and ultimately the ability to judge at all, fall into disuse because "surely, when the whole world shall have been genialized, it will be as out of place to talk of murderers, as in a Christianized world to talk of sinners" (199). No thoughtful Christian will miss the false notion of "a Christianized world". No reader who has followed Melville thus far will believe that not talking about murderers in a genialized world means that there will be none. Under the reign of Geniality sincerity is no longer a value because it is associated with sobriety, the search for truth, the desire to know. Geniality prefers easy acceptance and adoption of "a character".

The notion of playing a part is structurally important in this third group of encounters. Ventriloquism abounds as different characters either pretend to be acting for others or else tell stories in words other than their own. The characters of Melville's fiction begin acting out parts for each other in full view, of course, of the reader. Some motivations are reasonably clear on the level of interaction between characters. For example, the elaborate encounter between the cosmopolitan and the hail-fellow-well-met called Charlie Noble opens with Charlie recounting a long story about Colonel John Moredock and Indian-hating using the words, as he says, of Judge James Hall. When the cosmopolitan genially refuses to find Indian-hating credible (hate of anything has no place in his religion), Charlie Noble scrambles to reaffirm whatever his listener says. We can understand the utility to Charlie of using another's words: he can disavow them at any moment. Charlie Noble behaves like a confidence man acting a part, albeit on a provincial scale that points up the greater sophistication of the cosmopolitan.

The relation of apparent character to real character takes a further twist when Charlie leaves only to be followed by a messenger of distrust who warns the cosmopolitan that Charlie has been pointed out to him as probably a Mississippi con man. As is suitable for a satiric portrait of an Emersonian philosopher, Mark Winsome appears full of windy generalizations, irrelevant erudition, and contradictions. These latter, however, reveal Winsome condemning himself along with all others as equivocal characters. First he announces that Charlie is a con man because he, like all other snakes in nature, bears a label, available to be read. Moments later he affirms the contrary, that all are unknowable, including himself: " 'What are you? What am I? Nobody knows who anybody is. The data which life furnishes, towards forming a true estimate of any being, are as insufficient to that end as in geometry one side given would be to determine the triangle.' " (216) As dubious a mouthpiece as Mark Winsome may be, there is nothing in the behaviour of any of the characters in this section to say him nay. Even the cosmopolitan is not consistent in his professed geniality, thereby suggesting that it was just a friendly part he chose to play at the picnic of life. When his geniality is challenged, he drops that mask for the more sinister one of a necromancer, once rather light-heartedly with Charlie Noble, a second time more ominously to close this series by magically overpowering the distrust of William Cream, the barber. In the final chapter the cosmopolitan will adopt still another character.

Small wonder that the reader is likely to concur when Winsome's disciple Egbert, after elaborate role-playing with the cosmopolitan Frank Goodman, has recourse to Jacques' all-the-world's-a-stage speech from *As You Like It* and declares himself "at a loss to determine where exactly the fictitious character had been dropped, and the real one, if any, resumed" (253). The notion of a "real character" within a fiction devoted to multiple pretenses deserves special attention shortly. For the moment it may suffice to point out that even ignoring momentarily that these characters all exist within a fiction, the notion of a *real* character presumes the notion of consistency based on sincerity or some similar glue holding together the outer and inner person. The cosmopolitan has renounced such restraints from the beginning of his time on stage so that he in effect has no "real" self but only a series of speeches and actions visible to the reader. He employs these roles in encountering several others who seem comparably fictitious in the sense that they rarely play "themselves" but only more or less consciously adopted roles.

From the reader's point of view, then, this third series can only compound the confusion. The concept of confidence has become more abstract, more philosophical, but the characters who embody it, or its opposite, are the more various, shifting, inconclusive. The reader can watch the various characters adopt temporary masks but can never see them clearly unmasked.

There remains one final chapter to culminate the reader's mystification: "The Cosmopolitan Increases in Seriousness." Surely if there is a final resolution to the concatenation of shifting appearances, it should appear in the last chapter. About midnight on this April Fool's Day the cosmopolitan enters the gentleman's cabin where one aged man is awake, a Simeon-like reader of the Bible, who according to the narrator is not worldly wise but worldly ignorant, though his resistance to the cosmopolitan's religion of Geniality and Confidence shows him wary and worldly cautious none the less.

The old man recapitulates the main groups of "victims" who have preceded him. He professes an easy orthodoxy reminiscent of the first group who contributed money. When the cosmopolitan ponders how a passage describing confidence men could exist in the Bible with its message of hope and good news (literally, the Gospel), the old man resolves the difficulty by identifying the source of the passage as the Apocrypha, implying thereby that he need not deal with the notion at all.

On the other hand, the old man acts with a distrust of the creatures around him that is reminiscent of the second group of "victims", the unfortunates. Like them he wants evidence which would allow him to separate the real from the fake in the world around him. Hence he not only buys a stateroom lock from a worldly wise young peddler, but he eagerly sets about using a Counterfeit Detector the boy has given him as a bonus for his distrustful investment in the lock. But he discovers as convincingly as does the patient in Section Two that the counterfeit detector does not adequately evaluate the material he has in hand. He does not even consider the additional problem that the detector was made by someone whose motives are unknown and hence equivocal. The possibility of a counterfeit counterfeit detector is more than he can grasp.

Professing trust in the Creator and acting with distrust of the created, the old man is patently schizoid, thereby demonstrating another response to the problems developed in the third series of encounters. Up to this point the tensions between appearance and reality of evil and good have been resolved by eliminating one of the two terms, either the cosmopolitan's geniality or Winsome's distrust. The old man avoids the tension through a philosophical schizophrenia so thorough that he has lost all notion of connecting idea and fact: he gratefully accepts a chamber-pot given him by the cosmopolitan as satisfying his need for a "life-preserver". ("You could have confidence in that stool for a special providence." 285)

The cosmopolitan, as one possessing "indifferent eyes", "kindly" leads the old man to his stateroom, money belt and "life-preserver" in hand. Debate could go on endlessly about whether "kindly" should be understood ironically or straightforwardly. The evidence to decide the case is as unsure as any other counterfeit detector offered in this fiction. In the words of the final sentence: "Something further may follow of this Masquerade." Perhaps so, but the sense in which it has been a masquerade has never been clarified; the masquers never drop their disguises to reveal any "real" selves. Whatever may follow is in no way determined by what came before, any more than any plot incident has made its successor predictable.

The cosmopolitan is the grand-scale embodiment of confidence who seems little interested in the "friendly loans" he solicits. He proclaims the religion of easy optimism and trust in appearances but need not finally convince his interlocutors in order to make the inescapability of confidence clear. Pitch, Mark Winsome, his disciple Egbert, William Cream the barber, and the Simeon-like old man all resist his ministrations, yet all are ultimately subject to confidence in something, even if it be distrust. Thus the cosmopolitan as figure for the abstract principle of confidence does finally rule this April Fool's Day because all those involved must commit their confidence in one direction or another. The reader, unless he has been very circumspect, has likely succumbed to the same temptation.

The reader's case is finally the crucial one since the unresolved masquerade is created for his benefit and Melville has reserved three important chapters for direct commentary by the narrator about the nature of fictions, including this work. The result, rather than clarifying the issues, extends uncertainty to the aesthetic and metaphysical realms. Thus the opening of a direct relationship between the narrator and the reader results less in a clarification of the events in what he calls "the comedy of action" than an explanation of why they cannot be clear: "the comedy of thought".

These three intrusions of the narrator bear circular, self-cancelling titles which implicitly advertise how little clarification they will yield. Chapter XIV, the longest of the three, entitled "Worth the Consideration of Those To Whom It May Prove Worth Considering", treats literature primarily as a means to knowledge. Chapter XXXIII, "Which May Pass for Whatever It May Prove To Be Worth", touches mostly on literature as entertainment.

45

Chapter XLIV introduces factors of literary evaluation under a still more laborious title. Taken together, these interventions offer to condition the reader's intellectual understanding of the problems posed him by the narrative proper.

The first and most developed of these chapters is important because it is specifically tied to the narrative. At the close of Chapter XIII, Henry Roberts, the Good Merchant, has shed his conventional optimistic self to assert that truth is hard and suffering real (see above p. 38). The narrator then takes it upon himself, still employing his habitual evasive style, to offer an elaborate apology to an imagined reader who objects to the apparent inconsistency in this character. Since other characters, notably the man with a weed, have already changed more radically and "inconsistently" without drawing comment from the narrator, it is clear that Melville has manufactured a pretext for enlarging the reader's awareness of radical ambiguity.

Up to this chapter the reader must cope as he can with ambiguity on the level of action and character. Here about one-third into the work he encounters an abstract discussion of indeterminacy as endemic to this piece of fiction and, indeed, all fictions. The fundamental point insisted on by Melville's spokesman is that all creations impose ultimate doubts on their would-be interpreters. Literary characters, he maintains, are subject to two legitimate demands: internal consistency and truth to reality. Yet "reality" itself exhibits continual and surprising inconsistencies: "If reason be judge, no writer has produced such inconsistent characters as nature herself has" (77). The key here is the assimilation of nature to the writer. Both are creators and this novel as a creation shares with the work of the grand author of nature, the "author of authors" in Melville's draft of this chapter (387), a final inscrutability. The lesser author of the novel merely remains faithful to the imponderables created by his superior. The narrator favours those who say "of human nature the same that, in view of its contrasts, is said of the divine nature, that it is past finding out" (77). Thus the responsibility for the inconsistencies and the ambiguities of this text is transferred to the divine author of the book of nature.[9]

Even outside literature man's capacity for knowing "the facts" is inescapably limited. The narrator proposes that the best test for

46

knowledge is experience, which he then reveals to be unsatisfactory. One can never trust experience because humans cannot have infinite experience on which to base trustworthy knowledge:

> Experience is the only guide here; but as no man can be co-extensive with *what is*, it may be unwise in every case to rest upon it. When the duck-billed beaver of Australia was first brought to England, the naturalists, appealing to their classifications, maintained that there was, in reality, no such creature; the bill in this specimen must needs be, in some way, artificially stuck on.
>
> (77, Melville's italics)

In the sense that human beings derive categories from their experience which they then use to "make sense" of it, the narrator is quite right. One can never be certain that he is not encountering something new under his sun, a kind of platypus which escapes his previous categories. One can imagine, for example, a young man setting out into the world without ever having encountered a confidence man or the idea of one. Once he has witnessed the consistently inconsistent behaviour of a con man changing his pitch for successive victims, he can add the notion of such an operator to his map of human possibilities. Though he will then presumably be less eager to trust that human beings are always what they seem, the possibility exists that he may encounter a still more sophisticated duck-bill, perhaps someone who acts as a confidence man but beneficently. The regress is potentially infinite as the narrator makes clear. He who decides at any point that he knows the whole range of human variety accepts an arbitrary and incomplete framing of experience; in so doing he implies that his experience and knowledge approach the divine.

The transfer of responsibility for final uncertainty and equivocation from the author of this fiction to the author of the world sets the context for Melville's two later ventures into the "comedy of thought". In Chapter XXXIII the narrator proposes an analogous linking of the two worlds: "It is with fiction as with religion: it should present another world, and yet one to which we feel the tie" (207). Given Melville's postulation of the ultimate uncertainty of the divine and created nature, this fiction, *The Confidence Man*, fulfills the dictum both admirably and perversely. The perversity lies in the strict fidelity of this fiction to a world which is viewed as radically ambiguous because of the captiousness of the author of the book of the world. The reader will find no comforting fictions which imply a comprehensible reality outside fiction. In fact, since all existence has been conceived as fictive, the best he can do is learn to enjoy what he can in the comedy of action as well as that of thought.

There is one other alternative—one might compare diverse fictions in order to place this one in the context of literature, i.e. fiction conceived narrowly rather than all inclusively. Melville does this in the next-to-last chapter whose slight bulk of "smoky" discourse bears an incongrously long, self-cancelling and self-parodying title: "In Which the Last Three Words of the Last Chapter Are Made the Text of Discourse, Which Will Be Sure of Receiving More or Less Attention from Those Readers Who Do Not Skip It" (270).

The last three words of the preceding chapter are "QUITE AN ORIGINAL" (269, capitals in original), words that the barber and his friends apply to the cosmopolitan Frank Goodman in evaluating his ability as a charmer. By an elaborate dissertation on literary judgment, the narrator purports to show how the cosmopolitan is unworthy of the epithet "original" in comparison with Hamlet, Don Quixote, and Milton's Satan. But Melville has not introduced the very highest literary standards of comparison simply to punish his own creation. He raises the subject rather like the trial lawyer who proposes a line of questioning which he knows will be struck from the official record but will stay in the minds of the jury. The effect of the chapter is nothing less than to suggest that Melville has indeed created a genuinely original character worthy of comparison with the greatest originals in Western literature.

The narrator's approach to such a startling suggestion is carefully ironic. He begins by labelling most "original" characters as only superficially so in comparison to Hamlet and his fellows. A true original has certain, albeit rather vague, characteristics: he is as much of a prodigy in literature "as in real history is a new law-giver, a revolutionizing philosopher, or the founder of a new religion" (271). Also by definition he transcends the local in time or place. Thus far Melville's cosmopolitan (or his "confidence man" if one takes all the putative con men to be manifestation of a single "character") fits the criteria remarkably well: the cosmopolitan

48

surely transcends the local and he offers the world a new religion of geniality.

But the narrator continues with excessive modesty to devalue the role of the author's imagination in the creation of the truly "original" character: "But for new, singular, striking, odd, eccentric, and all sorts of entertaining and instructive characters, a good fiction may be full of them. To produce such characters, an author, beside other things, must have seen much, and seen through much: to produce but one original character, he must have had much luck" (271). Why luck? Because authors get their truly original characters not from imagination but from life: "There would seem but one point in common between this sort of phenomenon in fiction and all other sorts: it cannot be born in the author's imagination—it being as true in literature as in zoology, that all life is from the egg" (271). The narrator is, as usual, literally accurate: the proposition "all life is from the egg" is equally true in both literature and zoology, that is, it is unverifiable in both. Besides this obfuscation the narrator is begging the larger question he pretended to resolve earlier: the nature of "life" from which the author might have the "luck" to draw a genuinely original character. If literature is artifice, so after all is nature, created by the Great Artificer, presumably using His imagination if we can judge on the analogy of human authors. Of course we humans cannot know if we can trust our analogies and this is precisely the point of this entire piece of fiction. "Reality" has been shown to be as unknown and unknowable as fiction. In short, the narrator's dissertation on originality has contributed nothing of substance but has planted the standard of comparison Melville aspires to. In addition Hamlet, Don Quixote and Milton's Satan are more than monumental literary touchstones. Each is compelled by a vision of reality whose trustworthiness they themselves and we as readers are obliged to question. Once again confidence is the crucial issue.

The remarkable success of *The Confidence Man* is its uncanny ability to combine rational consistency with radical ambiguity. As the putative con men are to the characters they accost, so is the narrator to the reader, and so is the Creator to humankind: all present appearances are created on the basis of motives unknown, unknowable, and hence equivocal. What we call "reality"

49

outside of literature is simply a larger-scale fiction as indeterminate as this novel. Reality is finally appearance or, better, artifice. Those who try to penetrate appearances on any of the three levels face the same limitations in knowledge: suspicious hints but inadequate evidence, suggestive but inconclusive metaphors, opposing but uncompelling commitments of faith. If such is the nature of reality, we may have grounds for suspicion of those on any of the three levels who deny the presence of artifice: apparent con men who want to override doubts as to the reality of their charities or remedies; a narrator who plays down the role of imagination in fiction; a God who through the Bible encourages the Simeon-like old man to trust in the Creator while distrusting the created. But on all three levels there exist only grounds for suspicion. Those who have resolved these issues, the various cynical characters in each section or the cosmopolitan with his optimistic religion, have done so by committing their confidence in one position or the other but they gain no authority or truthfulness thereby. In order to act each must commit his confidence somewhere but Melville scrupulously pairs off inconclusive commitments against each other.

The "confidence man" of the title, then, is multiple. A number of characters (between eight and ten depending on one's reading) act rather like criminal confidence men soliciting money on diverse grounds. The more philosophical cosmopolitan preaches a religion of easy-going confidence in the reality of pleasant appearances. All are led in a dance by the idea of confidence itself: they must make some commitment of their confidence about the nature of things, whether or not they remain conscious of the final arbitrariness of that commitment. The subtitle proves still more revealing: the whole, like life in Melville's mature view, is an elaborate masquerade in which any unmasking only reveals a further mask. Even the most attentive reader will find himself, like the character Egbert, "at a loss to determine where exactly the fictitious character had been dropped, and the real one, if any, resumed" (253). Characters and readers, like all humankind, lack means to determine what is the real nature of things, if any.

NOTES

1. Uncertainty about the number of presumed confidence men is one of the several embarrassments of critical commentary on this work. A good deal of critical ink was splattered about in the 1950s in a fruitless attempt to decide if there were separate characters who shared a confidence spirit or if a single character was to be understood as disguising himself in a variety of ways. In recent years most critics have tended to presume the latter understanding despite the fact that the textual evidence is so inconclusive as to leave the question more properly described as moot. R. W. B. Lewis's position is representative when he concludes that there are eight avatars of the central character who are "the so-to-speak genuine masks of the Confidence Man". He comes to this conclusion by attributing inconsistencies either to unverifiable guile in one of the characters or to Melville's forgetfulness. This is by no means the only case of a critic feeling so uneasy with the inconclusiveness of Melville's text that he imports evidence to pin it down. See *Trials of the Word* (1965), 67.
2. Starting with Elizabeth Foster in her copiously annotated Hendricks House edition (1954), a number of critics have hoped to resolve Melville's equivocations by accumulating careful analyses of allusions. This technique, which has proved fruitful for advancing interpretation of *Moby Dick*, comes a cropper here where there is no internally defined context of meanings sufficient to confirm the critic's preferred frame of reference. This problem, for example, plagues H. Bruce Franklin's *The Wake of the Gods* (Stanford, 1963) and his annotations for the Bobbs-Merrill edition of *The Confidence Man* (1967). Melville himself carefully undercuts the truth value of analogies in having his narrator cast doubt on Pitch's "reasoning" (see above, p. 40).
3. See *Trials of the Word* (1965), 71.
4. For a recent example see Susan Kuhlmann, *Knave, Fool and Genius* (1973), which blandly assumes the culpability of the apparent con operators.
5. Richard Boyd Hauck, in *A Cheerful Nihilism: Confidence and "The Absurd" in American Humorous Fiction* (1971), p. 115, rightly states this proposition as Melville's consistent implication, though he too falls into the trap of imputing a truth value to certain analogies which seem "fallacious and absurd" (p. 123). Once again the critic and not the text supplies a definition of the *real* which condemns certain analogies as false where others remain convincing to him.
6. See, for one flagrant case, Merlin Bowen, "Tactics of Indirection in Melville's *The Confidence Man*", *Studies in the Novel*, 1 (Winter, 1969), 401–20, esp. 403. Bowen endorses the cynical view put forth in the early chapters by a one-legged cynic who denounces the putative confidence men. Whereas Bowen and others accept his view as the truth, he is one of the few characters who is proved wrong within the text

51

itself. He does not believe that any of Black Guinea's friends and references are on board whereas they manifestly are—though we are still unable to determine with certainty whether or not they are con men. (See *CM*, p. 13.)

7. In "Puns and Radical Ambiguity in Melville's *The Confidence Man*", *American Transcendental Quarterly*, No. 22, pt. 3 (Spring 1974), 91–5.

8. Starting with Elizabeth Foster in 1954 critics have tended to find in Pitch a trustworthy representative of their own faith in rationality. As an example of how usually sensible critics can become trapped in indefensible projections see Paul Brodkorb, Jr., *"The Confidence Man*: The Con Man as Hero"*, Studies in the Novel*, 1 (Winter 1969), 424, where he accepts the truth value of Pitch's analogies and some of those used by the PIO man because as analogies they are "quite true". This in the face of Melville's narrator who calls Pitch's analogies into question quite as much as all others.

9. My discussion of these chapters owes a considerable amount to Edgar Dryden's *Melville's Thematics of Form* (1968), which was the first to carry out consistently Melville's implications on the level of characters, readers and humanity. See pp. 150–95 passim.

3

André Gide and Hierarch
as Con Man

"What a fool is Honesty, and Trust, his sworn brother, a very
simple gentleman." Think of that. Trust, that is, confidence—
that is, the thing in this universe the sacredest—is rattlingly pronounced just the simplest.

—Melville, *The Confidence Man*

Melville's presentation of the confidence man and André Gide's
in *Les Caves du Vatican* (1914) share one important literary characteristic—both use an anonymous narrator who reports his observations of the encounters between confidence men and victims.
There the resemblance abruptly ceases. Where Melville's narrator
is serious and sombre, Gide's is lighthearted and offhand. Melville's
narrator addresses his reader to pass responsibility for his impre-
cisions off onto the nature of things and the Creator. Gide's is
always ready to drop his narrative to recount a family genealogy
back to the sixteenth century, to specify the pronunciation of a
proper name, or to titillate his reader with a chatty rhetorical
question. Melville's is uncertain and serious, Gide's is omniscient
and casual. These differences are important because they signal
Gide's radically different exploitation of the observer's slant on a
confidence situation. Because Melville's reader is ultimately unsure
whether or not he is dealing with con men, the implications are
essentially epistemological. Gide leaves no uncertainty at all and
shifts the interest to the moral evaluation or, more precisely,
moral revaluation of the confidence man.

Because Gide stays firmly within the confines of this world,
the issue of appearance versus reality shifts down from the meta-

physical to the mundane. The Pope may be God's representative on earth, but Gide limits his concern to this-worldly manipulations of His name and station. Gide's narrator is free to go behind the scenes to reveal the fakery of the con men and the posturing of the polite world. The primary result is a debunking of the complex of values associated with respectability. Gide can count on his con man seeming reprobate once his machinations are revealed from inside. What he adds is a view of middle-class and liberal values which drags them down to the same level. By these inverse means, then, the con man is decriminalized once he seems no more worthy of condemnation than those the world perceives as upright. Thus the con man who would once have appeared devilish now embodies one alternative life pattern no more and no less corrupt than the bourgeois notions held up to admiration in Gide's society and ours.

In part to defuse the potentially explosive social and moral issue implicit in his work, Gide keeps everything lighthearted and offhand. Presented straightforwardly such ideas could only be shocking to his audience. Indeed the controversy since 1914 about the anti-moral morality of Lafcadio's *"acte gratuit"* indicates that the disquieting implications came through quite sufficiently.[1] Gide labelled the work a *"sotie"*, literally a "foolery", thereby evoking a late medieval genre close to the farce. In it a group of acrobatic fools typically disobey, insult and finally disrobe an allegorical figure representing *"Le Monde"*, thereby showing the world and its conventions to be as foolish as they. The genre suits Gide admirably because it dramatizes his theme while permitting a wide range of satirical targets from the French Academy and the piously Catholic upper classes to the conventional fiction of his time, both sentimental and realistic. *Le Monde* is represented by three characters, each in turn lending his name to the first three of Gide's five "books" or chapters. Anthime Armand-Dubois is a freemason scientist out to reduce all life processes to explanation by tropisms. Julius de Baraglioul, Establishment novelist, devotes most of his energy, plus his aristocratic Church connections, towards election to the Academy. Finally, Amédée Fleurissoire, as tender as his feminine name, is fated to die while trying to carry out his self-appointed knight-errant's mission to right Rome's ills. With charming but significant improbability the three are all brothers-in-law. By the end of the third book Gide's reader has had ample opportunity to watch the worldly character types make fools of themselves as well as being victimized by the con men. Then Gide is ready to centre the fourth book on them, *"Le Mille-Pattes"*, the millipede-like band led by Protos, whose name is sufficient to suggest his prowess at dissimulation and disguise. Only then, when the two camps have exposed their positions, does Lafcadio take over the last chapter to evaluate them as alternatives. Sure enough, both appear equally ridiculous and he seeks a third alternative.

The "foolery", then, runs its appropriate course. Calling it a *"sotie"* has presumably helped to forestall criticism that the piece is not a proper "novel", as Gide suggests in his dedicatory letter,[2] but above all the gamesomeness of the form has allowed the author to toy with some radically untraditional notions. As we shall see, Gide's targets are concentrated in the three brothers-in-law who dramatize three major dimensions of the respectable bourgeois world: the intellectual (Anthime), the social (Julius) and the moral (Amédée). By imposing family links among them, however improbable they may be, Gide is suggesting a commonality in bourgeois conceptions which combine to form a unified world view for *Le Monde*. The genre, then, serves to sugar-coat the pill with fun. Equally important is Robert Alter's praise of the novel for its self-conscious probing of literary as well as social conventions: "Since this is a novel about how the literary imagination constructs reality, the parodistic set pieces and the use of parody as a model for character are not just playful self-indulgences but strictly functional explorations through the exaggeration of convention into what is hidden or revealed by convention."[3]

But to the con game itself, which is near classic in design and execution. In the guise of a priest or canon, likely carrying a handwritten introduction from a well known Cardinal, Protos approaches wealthy, conservative, credulous French Catholics with the startling revelation that the true Pope is imprisoned in the cellars of the Vatican—whence Gide's title. The false Pope, supported by an unholy alliance between freemasons and Jesuits, is responsible for such infamous declarations as Leo XIII's request that the aristocrats support the Third Republic in France.[4] Since the victims had already found that papal position an incredible affront to their inherited position in society, they eagerly accept the idea of imprisonment. Thus they readily co-operate in Protos' undercover crusade to liberate the "true Pope". Unlike the classic con game, this set-up does not require the victim to seek profit by assenting to an avowedly illegal scheme, but Protos' appeal to self-serving credulity is not far removed. The victims can feel holier than the "Pope" at the same time that they serve their own political, social, and economic interests.

Protos' scheme is brilliantly self-contained. Naturally the established hierarchy of the Church could not acknowledge the falsity of the Pope: it would discredit the Church as a whole and lead to still further erosion of ecclesiastical influence. Therefore the holy crusade must be kept secret even from local churchmen lest they unwittingly reveal to corrupt officials in Rome that the imposture is known. Thus the victims have no sources of information about the false Pope except what the gang provides.

When a knight-errant like Fleurissoire comes along wanting to contribute his personal service rather than funds, he can be drawn into the game by a standard con man's device already hinted at in Melville. By emphasizing the existence of widespread fraud in the Church hierarchy, the con men appear honest in their appeal for secrecy, more honest than those who claim there is no fraud. Thus Protos produces for Fleurissoire a bogus cardinal and canon who seem obliged to act in unholy fashion in order to escape the surveillance of the corrupt regular clergy. Once imposters seem to be everywhere, Amédée trusts only those who have introduced him to the idea of imposture.

To protect against possible exposure the gang is organized on a grand scale. In Rome there is the headquarters convenient to the Castel St. Angelo where the Pope is supposed to be imprisoned. In the house we find secret passages, an apparently inexhaustible supply of costumes, and Protos' mistress, Carola Venitequa, who is ready to wheedle information from newcomers who think they are in a hotel. The mail of visitors to Rome can be read. On the rail line between Rome and Naples Protos can proudly announce that the dining-car waiter as well as an intriguing widow with red stockings under her mourning clothes and her young daughter are all operatives. The organization is so omnipresent and efficient as to be unbelievable. In the caricatural and inconsecutive world of the *"sotie"* even that fact plays its part in the dénouement.

The motives that guide the "millipede" gang are those of any group of con men: *esprit de corps*, love of the game itself, and, of course, eagerness for the fees Protos exacts for confirming the fantasies of his victims. But Gide also allows us to glimpse a con man in formation by reporting something of Protos during his adolescence. During several schoolboy years Protos had considerable influence over Lafcadio, always attacking the conventional notion of sincerity. Protos' principle is that one should never appear to others as he really is. Not content with appearing merely ordinary in school, Protos wanted to be thought stupid. When others mistook or ignored him, he was free to pursue his own dark purposes. The daily practice of insincerity requires training and self-discipline, of course, but these are no problem for Protos whose passion for the game, its rigors and risks and rewards, is unbounded. Besides himself he also controls his organization with an unsentimental hand. He tries to blackmail Lafcadio into following his orders and the reader is invited to suppose that he holds similar levers over his other operatives.

As a schoolboy Protos already divided the world into two camps: the *"subtils"* and the *"crustacés"*. Protos, needless to say, is the prototype of subtlety who has no stable self to present to the world. In the succession of identities he assumes the only common ground is his motivation to dominate and bilk those around him. The *"crustacés"* are the conventional individuals, the squares, who make their way through life by secreting a thick protective carapace comparable to those of crabs and lobsters. The exoskeleton which fixes their stable identities is of course also their trap and limitation. Superficially different as Gide's three principal *"crustacés"* are, they are equivalent in their commitment to a bourgeois morality, a philosophical-religious position and a social standard which prove excessively rigid and ultimately empty.

Anthime Armand-Dubois, the freemason scientist, is Gide's portrait of the bourgeois crustacean as intellectual. He dramatizes the preposterousness of bourgeois pretense that the world can be reduced to a simple and unitary explanation. Anthime begins as an aggressively atheistic scientist out to prove that all nature depends on a few simple tropisms. As a caricature of the scientist, he naturally denies the existence or importance of emotions despite the annoying counter-evidence of a large wen which began growing behind his ear after his marriage. When the magic world of the *"sotie"* permits a miraculous cure of the wen, Anthime changes into a repentant sinner and a devout member of the Church. He has changed as a crustacean molts, shedding one exoskeleton for another equally rigid. Faith replaces rational inquiry; he is confident of being attuned to the simple truth, spiritual in nature, embodied in the Church, visible in the Pope.

Gide is not content to mock Anthime with this single molting. When he hears that the Pope in the Vatican may be an imposter, he suddenly reverts to this atheist's views. If the Pope can be the wrong one, then so can the Heaven for which the Pope is the visible guarantee. Gide's implication is that it makes no significant difference whether Anthime professes Christianity or Atheism. The bourgeois trust in coherent and "rational" explanations is the chief target. Anthime's two brothers-in-law exemplify complementary facets of the same outlook.

Julius de Baraglioul, the most central of Gide's crustaceans, epitomizes the bourgeois as pragmatic social climber. The possibility that the Pope might be an imposter does not bother him. The Church for him is a pragmatically useful organization which guarantees his respectability and advances his worldly interests. If others in pursuing their own self-interest go so far as to imprison the true Pope, that is only an extension of the way Julius usually thinks and acts.

The ruling ambition of Julius' life is to be elected to the French Academy. To this end he musters support among the Church hierarchy in France plus aristocratic family connections and, incidentally, he writes novels. His works are as respectable, pallid, and dull as he. Since he has no inner life of his own, he cannot create a character who does. His latest novel depicts the publicly visible shell of his father's life as a French diplomat. Unfortunately, however, Julius has not imagined Count Juste-Agenor as capable of a private emotional life; hence it is a jolt to discover that his father has had an illegitimate son, one Lafcadio, who is thus his own half-brother. Because Julius has taken the appearances of public life so naïvely, so literally, his book is a failure with the critics and, still worse, with his father as well.

Julius never sheds completely his exoskeleton of respectable self-interest, though the advent of Lafcadio coupled with the failure of his book does inspire some movement towards molting. For a time he excitedly explores the idea of a character who, like Lafcadio and unlike himself, has escaped from catechism, conformity, calculation. (*"Echappée au catéchisme, à la complaisance, au calcul"* 817). But Julius can never free himself from conformity and self-seeking calculation. Even in the midst of his imagining a gratuitously criminal character, a type we will examine shortly, Julius' excitement is reserved for the vision of himself, noble and daring at last, giving the Academy a morality shocking enough to justify their having turned him down.

If Julius epitomizes the social ambition of the middle class, Amédée Fleurissoire bumblingly acts out its moral self-image. He is a caricature of self-denying nobleness. Having beaten his bosom friend and rival for the hand of their common love, he feels obliged to refrain from consummating the marriage. When he hears of the Vatican caper, he immediately dons what Stephen Dedalus calls the "spiritual-heroic refrigerating apparatus, invented and patented in all countries by Dante Alighieri", i.e. his exoskeleton embodying his vision of himself as a crusader in shining armour. If only Fleurissoire would stay in the quiet provinces of Southwestern France, his life could go on its undisturbed self-denying way. But taking his masochistic self-image so literally, he feels obliged to go directly to Rome to offer his help. By the same token he is totally unequipped to cope with the multiple disharmonies between appearance and reality that await him there.

Amédée's crusade to Rome to liberate the Pope humourously re-enacts the plagues suffered by many a medieval knight; he endures bedbugs (Marseilles), fleas (Toulon), and mosquitoes (Genoa) before arriving in the heavenly city. But steadfast in his mission, he goes on trusting in the trappings of the Vatican plot carefully mounted for him by Protos and his gang. In fact, Protos lead Amédée such a merry chase in and out of disguises and mutual pretenses that the poor man is happy to relax on the train from Rome to Naples, where he is to deliver six thousand francs for "the cause". Always conscientious, he leaves one compartment because an Italian appears threatening to him. He settles down across from a well dressed young man whose face appears pleasant. He relaxes there in the presence of Lafcadio, who for thoroughly private reasons we will examine in a moment, pushes him out of the moving train a few minutes later. The appearances have done him in, though as Maurice Geracht points out, this instance of his trusting appearances has been fatal only by chance.[5] Fortunately Gide keeps this portrait of the perfect simpleton from falling into sentimentality by the use of dramatic irony. Since the reader always knows just how wrong Fleurissoire is in his judgments, his blunders fit into the *"sotie"* atmosphere as more laughable than pitiable.

These three caricatured types admirably represent the conventional bourgeois world that a *"sotie"* holds up to ridicule. The nature of the con men we have seen already. There remains one crucial character to consider—Lafcadio, the young man with a foot in either camp who is apparently faced with a choice between joining one or the other. Though formally speaking the narrator remains as detached as before, by focusing the final chapter on Lafcadio he sanctions the moral speculations that have the effect of revaluing the confidence man.

Lafcadio's freedom from the *"crustacés"* is implicit in his background. He has no regular parentage, no consistent schooling, no religion, no responsibilities, no uncontrollable wants. Even during his days of poverty in Paris he pays cash or does without. To point up his aristocratic but irregular upbringing, Gide fashions a succession of "uncles" who take up with his mother, each offering an influence retained in the mature Lafcadio. The list reads like a parody of European cultural stereotypes. The German, Baron Heldenbruck, insists that the boy Lafcadio perform mathematical marvels in his head and toughen his body with exposure to cold. His English uncle Faby, Lord Gravensdale, contributes a lighthearted homosexuality. The Italian, Baldi, with his endless mimicry and magic tricks, affirms that everything can be transformed by sleight of hand. Life is a game not to be taken seriously; one learns to play cards and simultaneously to cheat. Count Bielkowski, the Pole, instills the love of stealth and intrigue for their own sakes by leading the boy on an elaborately cautious foray to sneak a midnight glass of tokay from his own sideboard. The last uncle is French, the Marquis of Gesvres, who satisfies whims before bodily needs because whims might evaporate whereas hunger only becomes more intense the longer it is ignored. With this succession of influences behind him Lafcadio is a model of unconventionality. His father, Count Juste-Agenor, has in fact played no part in his upbringing and enters only to ackowledge his paternity with a death-bed legacy handsome enough to allow Lafcadio to live at last on the scale of his accumulated aristocratic impulses.

If from his uncles Lafcadio has learned largely impulsiveness and easy morality, he has also absorbed much of the self-control necessary to a con man during his adolescent apprenticeship to Protos. Lafcadio's account book records a period of intense schoolboy self-discipline for dissimulation inspired by Protos. The recorded failures are all similar in that they involve having let his feelings or his prowess come out into the open. For each lapse into some kind of sincerity Lafcadio punishes himself dramatically by plunging the point of a sharp knife into his thigh. Thus he inflicts on himself one "punta" for having beaten Protos at chess and hence revealed that he is the better player. Protos, we gather, is guilty of no actions that are not deliberate and calculated; Lafcadio had been his disciple as well as the willing pupil of his diverse uncles.

Lafcadio's conflicting impulses toward self-indulgence and self-control constitute a fundamental duality in his character that is significant in the climax of the story. He develops his notions through three major conversations. The first, between Lafcadio and himself, results in the murder of Fleurissoire. The second encounter, between Julius and Lafcadio, results in the latter's definitive break with the *"crustacés"*. Finally, Lafcadio refuses to join Protos' gang and thereby rejects the *"subtils"*.

Riding the compartment with Fleurissoire Lafcadio indulges in an elaborate internal dialogue turning around spontaneity. Curiosity invites him to push Fleurissoire out of their compartment door and then see what happens. His professed interest in the game of life is that things never turn out just as one expects and especially if one abhors boredom, certainty, and repetition, one must try out all sorts of impulses, not just "good" ones. Hence Lafcadio's final justification to himself for the crime is plenitude of impulses, all sorts: *"Que tout ce qui peut être soit!"* (823, "Let everything that can be be.")

Yet even the decision to commit murder must, if he is to be consistent, remain spontaneous and thus Lafcadio's strategy with himself is to cut off thoughts that might reach ahead to foresee the consequences of his action and thus contaminate it with calculation. His devices constitute a series of little games he plays with himself. He will push Fleurissoire out only if he sees a light in the passing countryside before reaching twelve in a slow count. His ideal is never to think ahead and hence never to be less than spontaneous in his own eyes.

Thus Lafcadio's justification for murder is essentially aesthetic (to see what consequences will follow from any impulsive action) and beyond any moral restrictions (no impulses are to be repressed). He is equally flexible and fastidious with the labels he applies to himself. He cannot think of himself as a criminal since crimes are committed for some motive. He prefers the notion *"aven-turier"* (833) since the term is as flexible morally as his beaver hat is physically. Similarly he refuses to appropriate the six thousand francs he finds in Amédée's coat since that would class him in his own eyes as a mere thief. But the "adventure" once embarked upon, Lafcadio cannot bring himself simply to leave, especially since he finds in Fleurissoire's pocket a railroad pass belonging to Julius. He returns to Rome.

Lafcadio is drawn to seek out Julius because, in spite of himself, he has a desire for recognition in the respectable world. He would like Julius to acknowledge him as a brother, at least in their personal conversation. Besides he has a childish curiosity to know how people are reacting to this non-criminal murder. For someone to appreciate how clever he has been he chooses Julius.

At first Lafcadio and Julius hit it off surprisingly well. Julius is excitedly imagining a new kind of character, a man free from concern with the consequences of his acts, able equally to commit actions considered criminal or saintly. Lafcadio, of course, is precisely that character himself and he delightedly joins in helping to sketch out his nature. It is one of those self-reflective situations dear to Gide when the fiction turns on itself to contemplate its own components. Melville would have enjoyed the situation as well. In fact, Julius, in criticizing the consistency and predictability of characters that have choked his previous novels, echoes arguments advanced by Melville's narrator in Chapter XIV of *The Confidence Man.*[6]

Alas Julius reverts to type at precisely the moment when he

encounters the real existence of the new character he has been imagining. The newspaper reports of Fleurissoire's death, instead of confirming his new notions, send him scurrying back into his pragmatic shell: the Pope must indeed be imprisoned and Amédées death motivated by his inside knowledge of the situation. The reaffirmation of Julius' uppercrust self is complete when news arrives of his election to the Academy. When Lafcadio later confesses the murder of Amédée, Julius remains coolly self-centred and Lafcadio's last ties to the *"crustacés"* are cut.

If aligning himself with the conventional types is out of the question, Lafcadio must still confront the other alternative, the *"subtils"*. Protos arranges that they meet on the train returning the body of Fleurissoire from Naples to Rome. Protos does not appear as himself of course but as a Professor of Criminal Law from Bordeaux, incidentally providing Gide with the occasion for a brilliant caricature of a meek, mincing provincial type. While the two are eating together, the "Professor" slips onto Lafcadio's plate a cufflink reported missing from Fleurissoire's body. Protos also has in his possession the maker's label from Lafcadio's hat which could expose his role in the death. Thus Protos is prepared to blackmail Lafcadio into working for him. He is less interested in money than in exacting obedience. Protos, after all, originated the division of the world into *"crustacés"* and *"subtils"*. He who breaks with the first automatically falls among the second: " *'Mais ce qui m' étonne, moi, c'est que, intelligent comme vous êtes, vous avez cru, Cadio, qu'on pouvait si simplement que ça sortir d'une société, et sans tomber du même coup dans une autre; ou qu'une société pouvait se passer de lois'* " (858). (" 'But what really astonishes me, Cadio, is that you, intelligent as you are, believed that one could so simply leave one society without falling by the same stroke into another; or that a society could get along without laws'.") But Protos fails to reckon with the depth to which Lafcadio remains faithful to the adolescent principles enunciated by Protos himself.

In his earlier discipleship to Protos, Lafcadio ingested two of the master's formulas: *"passer outre"*, which implies ignoring or overcoming all objections or restraints, and *"qu'à cela ne tienne"*, which in modern English idiom has the force of, "Why not?"[7] Both of these notions encourage evasion of external controls over the individual. Thus, partly with Protos' help, Lafcadio has come to hate all rules and external restraints, not just those of the bourgeois world. Also, even before their final meeting he has differentiated himself from the crudeness of Protos' drive for power. Riding on the train with Amédée, Lafcadio presumes that Protos has left to join *"les barbares de Chicago"*, already by 1914 reputed for its gangsters. Lafcadio sees in himself a finer, more aristocratic flowering.

Lafcadio is unwilling to serve the mature Protos because the latter seems indistinguishable from Julius. To Lafcadio both men and the groups they represent are controlled and limited by their concern for consequences. Protos happens to head a criminal organization, Julius to represent polite society, but neither is free in Lafcadio's sense of the word. Both are bound by goals, by calculation, by work directed toward power and success. The further ramifications of Lafcadio's preference for *"l'acte gratuit"* are not important in the present context because the essential decriminalization of Protos as confidence man is already clear. He is rejected not on legal or moral grounds but for offering no better alternative than conventional conformity!

In the narrative Lafcadio's refusal to serve Protos seems to dissolve the latter's control over his own world. He falls victim to the unforeseeable nonsequiturs that are at home in a *"sotie"*. Carola, assuming that Fleurissoire has been killed on orders from Protos, denounces him to the police. Protos, the master of self-control, strangles her in a rage and is arrested with the incriminating piece of Lafcadio's hatband in his possession. Hence Protos is incarcerated as a double murderer. He is the con man hoist with his own petard. Like the respectable crustaceans, he has been bound by the expectation that his "society" guaranteed a predictable and consistent framework for his values. But the gratuitous takes revenge on the causal. Only Lafcadio seems to escape, though the overriding context of "foolery" mitigates the seriousness of its implications.

It has been Lafcadio's book in several senses. His amoral aesthetic view of life dominates at the last just as the *"sotie"* as a form enforces the primacy of the unpredictable and spontaneous. Even the narrative structure reflects his values. Chapters do not begin where their predecessors left off and sections within chapters are often discontinuous. Plot and character reversals often seem as gratuitous and unmotivated as Lafcadio's crime. Gide, in fact, goes out of his way to mock the conventions of realistic fiction. In introducing Anthime's wen, for instance, the narrator elaborately feigns ignorance of which details are essential so that he can ironically proclaim how earnestly faithful to "reality" he is trying to be. This is Gide's chiding of the crustaceans among his readers, those who want their fiction to appear non-fictional. As Albert Guérard puts it, "few important novelists since the eighteenth century had intruded themselves so wilfully, or with such apparent disregard for illusion."[8] Both Gide as writer and his hero scorn the anti-aesthetic world of causal mechanism.

Gide, of course, extends such protests against the unreality of so-called real life in *The Counterfeiters* (1925), a work which is perhaps his greatest. There the exposure of multi-layered pretense in the lives of his characters plus the multiple layering of fictional modes dramatizes most memorably the artifice of the "real". *The Vatican Cellars*, however, remains the more important work in the present context. Here Protos brings the figure of a con man directly to bear in the assault on bourgeois values. And, as we shall see in succeeding chapters, the progressive use of the confidence figure to undermine traditional Western values begins, as does Gide, with the relatively visible public dimension of those values. Only later will the con man serve explicitly to subvert their more intimate manifestations.

In the present context Gide has, in effect, domesticated the confidence figure. Protos has certain demonic overtones in the way he manipulates others, but Satan suffers the same demeaning fate as God.[9] Their rivalry has shrunk to a conflict between Pope and anti-Pope, the latter being Protos himself, the head of another complex and worldly organization. It is only Protos' scheme that imprisons the Pope and sets himself up in parodic opposition, but none of the more pious characters finds it impossible to conceive chicanery within the hierarchy of the Church. Thus corruption is credible everywhere as metaphysical issues are domesticated and secularized into problems of social morality. In this sort of a moral environment the confidence man is decriminalized if not yet esteemed.

Gide's handling of point of view contributes importantly to this

C   65

step in revaluation. For the reader to accept the proposition that the con man is at least no worse than his victims—the classic claim of criminal con men—he must be able to see the manipulations from inside. Through his omniscient narrator Gide takes his reader at least partway behind the scenes. Hence, even though Protos is ultimately rejected by Lafcadio, the reader has been able to perceive his manipulations as comparable to those of the respectable fakers. A further step in exposing to the reader the con man's own point of view emerges in Thomas Mann's Felix Krull, who from his retirement will set about recounting and justifying his own career as a con man. With the freedom to narrate his own story, Felix can invite his reader to view the con game not simply as one life option among others but as an admirable service to humankind, as necessary and useful as that of the artist.

NOTES

1. For a rehearsal of the controversy surrounding this notion see James A. Grieve, "Lafcadio: A Reappraisal", *Australian Journal of French Studies*, 3 (1966), 22–35, esp. 29–32.

2. See André Gide, *Romans, Récits et Soties, Oeuvres Lyriques*, ed. Yvonne Davet et Jean-Jacques Thierry (Paris, 1958), 679. All further references to this standard text of *Les Caves du Vatican* will be indicated by page references in parentheses following quotations.

3. Robert Alter, *Partial Magic: the Novel as a Self-Conscious Genre* (1972), 162.

4. For a good history of the actual Vatican swindles to which Gide alludes see Alain Goulet, *Les Caves du Vatican d'André Gide: Etude Méthodologique* (Paris, 1972), esp. 155–73.

5. Maurice Aron Geracht, "A Guide Through the Vatican Caves: A Study of the Structure of *Les Caves du Vatican*", *Wisconsin Studies in Contemporary Literature*, VI (1965), 339.

6. Elizabeth Foster was the first to point out how closely Gide's mature conception of character approximates and echoes Melville's, though she concentrated on *Les Faux-Monnayeurs*, where these notions are more fully developed. See her notes to Melville's chapter XIV in her edition of *The Confidence Man* (New York, 1954), 316.

7. Dorothy Bussy's 1927 translation of this phrase as "What's the odds?" gives the inappropriate implication that the speaker is calculating possible outcomes. See Penguin edition of *The Vatican Cellars*, p. 80 or the Anchor edition, misleadingly entitled *Lafcadio's Adventures*, p. 91.

8. Albert J. Guérard, *André Gide* (New York, 1963), 137.
9. Graeme Watson links Protos with Goethe's Mephistopheles in the process of pointing out some of his devilish traits. See "Protos", *Australian Journal of French Studies*, 3 (1966), 16–21.

4

Thomas Mann and Everyman as Con Man

> A shoemaker; one whose calling it is to defend the understandings
> of men from naked contact with the substance of things: a very
> useful vocation.
>
> —Melville, *The Confidence Man*

Gide's *sotie* seems blatant and simple in comparison with the
multifoliate splendours of Mann's *Bekenntnisse des Hochstaplers
Felix Krull* (*The Confessions of Felix Krull, Confidence Man*, 1911,
1954).[1] It is impressive that Mann could add Books Two and
Three after a lapse of more than forty years yet leave hardly a
seam showing.[2] It is memorable that he could turn the figure of
the con man to such multiple comic and satirical account.

Already implicit in the title is the mating of the confidence
figure with the "true-confessions" genre which flowers in Mann's
comic imagination. Since a con man is *confessing*, the reader expects to see all sorts of dirty linen; since a *con man* is confessing,
the reader expects uncommonly interesting dirt, false identities,
illicit scrambles to rise in the world. But because a con man is
telling his own story, a suspicion lurks that he may manipulate
his reader in the same spirit as he tricks his victims. The way is
open to multiple satire, not only on the bourgeois world which
Felix Krull manipulates almost at will, but also on the world of
literature, which is similarly based on pretences. Fakery, from the
title on, is a crucial ground for the reader's engagement with the
story. When a story-teller advertises himself as a con man, how
can anything he says be trusted as "true"? Ultimately the work
implies that reality is too elusive to be genuinely confessable,

but Mann's comic genius keeps the tone light. The layering of his playful pretenses is complex and we need to peel open several internal frames of reference before it can become clear just how Felix Krull accomplishes a new extension of the confidence man in literature.

The place to begin my analysis is not at the beginning but at the innermost. I propose a frame analysis of the layers of imbedded pretense that Mann opens to his reader.[3] These layers are more easily perceived from the inside of the onion toward the outside because once Mann has made clear the kind of relationship that holds between picture (segment of narrative) and frame (circumstances of narration), he leaves undefined the limits of the outermost frame, the final size and shape of the onion. What I will be doing, then, is showing how picture is conditioned by frame which occurs in a larger picture which is conditioned in turn by its frame and so on. (See diagram overleaf.)

NARRATIVE LEVEL I: The innermost segment of narration in the novel occurs in Chapter IX of Book Three where Felix Krull, impersonating the Marquis Louis de Venosta of Luxembourg, encounters first the Luxembourg ambassador to Portugal and then King Don Carlos I himself. What defines this twenty-page episode as innermost is the framing of its narration. The reader does not "see" these incidents through Felix's habitual narrative eyes; instead he reads of them in a long letter addressed by "Venosta" to his parents back in Luxembourg. In it the parents are invited to admire the ease and cleverness with which "Venosta" handled himself with the nobility, the proof of his success being his receiving the Portuguese Order of the Red Lion, "second class" (the latter detail a brilliant touch by Mann).

FRAME I: The reader's perception of this incident, however, is inevitably coloured by his awareness of the circumstances controlling its creation. The letter is designed to reassure the Venosta parents that the world tour they planned for their son "Loulou" will successfully distract his thoughts away from his Paris showgirl, Zaza. The reader is invited to admire the skill with which "Venosta" throws his parents off the scent: how Professor Kuckuck's paleontological discourses are reported to engage "Venosta's" attention more than the Kuckuck ladies, how his activities in Lisbon are made to appear socially desirable from the parents'

69

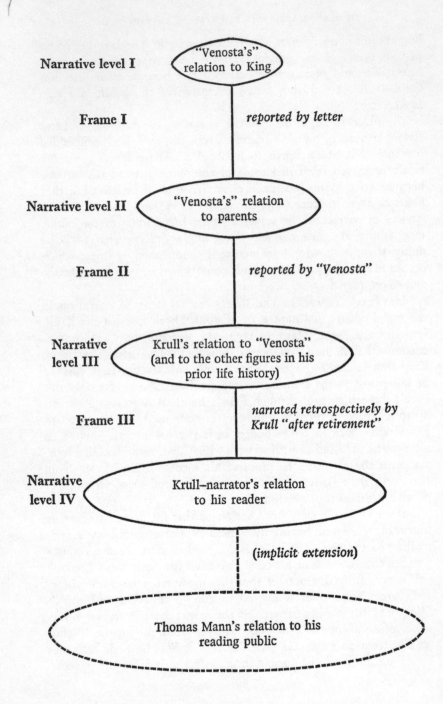

Narrative level I — "Venosta's" relation to King

Frame I — *reported by letter*

Narrative level II — "Venosta's" relation to parents

Frame II — *reported by "Venosta"*

Narrative level III — Krull's relation to "Venosta" (and to the other figures in his prior life history)

Frame III — *narrated retrospectively by Krull "after retirement"*

Narrative level IV — Krull–narrator's relation to his reader

(implicit extension)

Thomas Mann's relation to his reading public

point of view. The reader is immediately aware that the letter is a conscious fabrication designed to manipulate the parents. A moment's reflection would remind him that the wool may be pulled over his own eyes as well—to an unknowable extent since there is no report of the incident besides the letter.

NARRATIVE LEVEL II: This next larger frame of narrative reference, then, concerns the relations between "Venosta" and his parents. This context is prolonged by the reprinting of Mother Venosta's reply to her "son's" letter. She expresses cartainty that at least parts of the letter were made up: surely "Venosta" did not use the over-elegant phrases of flattery he reports, "That is certainly a letter-writer's fiction." (340) None the less she is greatly pleased with the report since it confirms her hopes. The reader, of course, can only smile because he is fully aware of the larger context within which this relationship is framed.

FRAME II: All the narrative we have examined so far has been reported by "Venosta", but the reader knows that "Venosta" is really Felix Krull. The events of the Krull-Venosta relationship, filling as they do the entire second half of the novel, culminate Felix's long-standing ambition to rise in the world. He will do so by trying to flesh out the trappings of Venosta's life as a young nobleman. If "Loulou" Venosta has a beauteous "Zaza" to love, then "Venosta" will seek out her counterpart in "Zouzou", whose name neatly merges the other two. He will even adapt Venosta's drawing of the nude Zaza in order to approximate his fantasies of Zouzou in the same state of undress. He is trying to live out, albeit with a wrongly chosen partner, the "double-image" that has been inspiring him since his youth in Frankfurt. Leaving aside the importance of the double-image for the moment, we can see none the less how the Krull-Venosta relationship climaxes the main movement of the Felix Krull story from his birth to his climactic mating with Dona Maria Pia Kuckuck on the eve of his scheduled departure from Lisbon for South America.

NARRATIVE LEVEL III. Everything that occurs on these two inner levels of narrative is conditioned in the reader's eyes by being embedded in Felix's life story. The goals manœuvres of Krull-Venosta "Make sense" only in the context of Felix's life progress, starting with his splendidly tawdry family life and the emergence of his will to con the world. Some readers may be tempted to take this conventional *bildungsroman* story as self-sufficient and self-explanatory. Sooner or later, however, we must acknowledge that the circumstances governing the narration themselves modify our relation to the events and our sense of their significance.

FRAME III: The whole Krull story is recounted by retrospective narration in the past tense, mounted by Krull-narrator at some rather vague time after his retirement. Thus, as narrator, Felix can announce important facts that occur after the closing of the narrative proper—his later arrest, for example. Also he steps aside from the narration to condition his reader's response to it. He is especially solicitous about maintaining not only a good opinion of Felix-Krull-character but also about his credibility as narrator. He opens with the true-confession frame *de rigueur* since Rousseau: he will tell all and he is to be trusted because he will recount unflattering as well as complimentary details about his earlier self. In point of genre-fact the lure of "confession" is precisely that it hints at acts unseemly enough to be interesting reading.

There is, of course, one further frame—behind Felix Krull as narrator there stands Thomas Mann, discreetly identified only on the title page. The relations between Mann and his reading public are implicitly modified by the publication of this book as his last in a weighty and distinguished production. These implications however, must wait till we see how Mann uses these nested narrative frames to order his multiple satirical thrusts.

On the level of Narrative I the target is the nobility. "Venosta", when he so easily wins not only acceptance but also honour within the royal court, exposes its hollowness in several ways. The nobles are boorish and boring even though they presumably have had the benefit of the education which is one of the classic justifications for the existence of their class. No one notices or cares when Felix praises to the king the castles of Sintra and the Monastery of Belem without yet having visited them. The hollowness of court flattery, as well as its utility, is neatly demonstrated.

Narrative level II similarly mocks the nobility but now in the context of "Venosta's" relations with his parents. In her reply Mother Venosta makes no criticism of his fabricated praise of buildings not yet seen; she tacitly acknowledges the acceptability of such pretenses in the life of her class. What she does choose to complain about is a matter of style: her "son's" excessive and unseemly elegance in the phrases he is reported to have used with the king. Still more ironically the good lady explains to herself the apparent improvement in her son's good looks by evoking the notion that "the desire to please can improve the exterior from within" (348). The reader, who already sees these events in the context of Narrative level III, can recognize here a reiteration of Felix Krull's chief explanation of why he with his seedy family and poor prospects turned out to be so handsome, skilled, and successful. He so loved the world that he formed himself in the light of its highest expectations. The moral trickery of the con man is thus recognized among the nobles as well. But these upper-class targets are easy marks and occupy little of Mann's time; there is more bite in Narrative level III.

On this level the character Felix Krull fulfils, as if magically, the urge toward social climbing that undergirds middle-class life. Thus Felix, by taking social appearances so seriously as to shape himself to ape his betters, dramatizes the realities of social hypocrisy. His very success demonstrates the hollowness of the life to which he and his bourgeois reader aspire. Mann makes the target humourously clear when he has Felix proclaim his fidelity to middle-class values like thrift. In Paris young Felix did not squander the proceeds of his thefts but instead opened a savings account at the Credit Lyonnais. Implicit is a wink of implied understanding that as long as the appearances are maintained, Felix presumes that his reader, in good middle-class fashion, will not worry too much about the source of the funds so carefully banked.

On occasion Felix openly appeals to the class prejudices of his bourgeois reader. As "Venosta" he wrote home in praise of distinctions between rich and poor which help to justify the upper class. As Felix he reports visiting a café with his working-class companion from the hotel, Stanko. The latter makes a mistake common to his class when he sets out to ape bourgeois fashion in his off hours. He and his fellows ought to know better (188). Also we must not forget that much of Felix's education in the upper world's ways comes from that classic fantasy fulfilment of the middle class—window shopping.

In Narrative frame III, Felix as narrator expresses elaborate concern for the acceptability of his book in the best homes. The satire is thus transferred to the literary tastes of the aspiring class. Felix as narrator plans to offer only the highest examples of literary style. He even announces that he is committing his confessions to paper in what he calls his own neat handwriting—safely invisible to readers of the printed book. The tone of the narrator's direct addresses to his reader is either fawning, as in the examples we have seen, or, on occasion, imperious.

Felix has additional fun with bourgeois hypocrisy when he adopts the high moral tone. Like Lafcadio before him he stretches language by creating a morally flexible term, "benervedness" (*"Benervung"*, 94), to replace "enervating" (*"entnervend"*), the unpleasantly clinical term for the effects of his prolonged sexual indulgence with Rosza. Felix manages to praise himself for the literary virtue of enriching German vocabulary. More coyly he chastises his reader for anticipating salacious passages in "confessions", asserting that there will be none of that here. His first sexual encounter emerges within a page. In effect Felix is titillating his middle-class reader with the expectations appropriate to the genre of confessions while at the same time underlining the pious tone and proper behaviour both narrator and reader are supposed to maintain.

With similar intent Felix announces early on that in his later career he was arrested and imprisoned. The bourgeois reader is thus assured that "justice" will reign in the end and hence he can settle back to enjoy the real business of "confessions": to tantalize and ultimately to placate him by following the imagined success of someone of humble origin who is freed by literature to indulge in manifold forms of the illicit.

Felix's posturing as narrator is itself a source of humour. It is overly elaborate and dated, even given the turn-of-the-century context. Mann is having fun with the pomposities of literature itself, including, by implication, much of his own earlier work. To see how these implications emerge, it is useful to watch him demolishing credibility on each narrative level. Mann undercuts each level of "truth" and with truth, out goes the seriousness of literature.

There are few problems on the two innermost levels of narrative because the reader is aware the "Venosta" is only Felix Krull. But he might pause over "Venosta's" admission to his mother that he dissembled before the king. Comparable self-exposures occur at the ensuing levels as well. After all, the only narrative authority for the encounter with the king is the letter itself, which the reader perceives from the outset as a fabrication of "Venosta". But "Venosta" is a fabrication of Felix Krull and Felix Krull is a fabrication of Krull-narrator. There is no authority to guarantee authenticity outside this—or any other—literary text.

The narrator himself worries over the problems of his writing to the point where he exposes his confessions themselves as consciously fabricated. The genre, as we have seen, promises veracity and also interesting revelations. Felix himself, speaking as narrator, remarks more than once on the problems of meeting simultaneously the claims of both. Truth, ideally, should appear spontaneously in a manner uncontaminated with artistry. By the start of Book Two, Felix the narrator is beginning to worry out loud about the problems of unselfconscious narration:

> For although I have often maintained that I am setting down these reminiscences principally for my own occupation and amusement, I will now honour truth in this respect, too, and admit freely that I have in secret and as it were out of the corner of my eye given some heed to the reading public as well; . . . I have had to decide whether these true recollections, conforming modestly to the facts of my life, could compete with the inventions of writers, especially for the favour of a public whose satiety and insensitivity—the result of such crass productions—cannot be exaggerated.   (53)

Five chapters later our narrator is genially admitting that he finally must employ the ruses, the delays and tricks that professional writers use for tension and dramatic interest. "Interest" has won out over truth.

Perhaps, by admitting that he has succumbed to "literary" tampering with the facts, Felix has none the less won the confidence of some readers with his candour in admitting that his confessions are more "literary" than true. If so, it will only be for those unconcerned with the pretense acknowledged and demonstrated by Felix Krull in the inner frames already examined. Pretence has proved an infinite regress undercutting all "truth value" in this text.

The implied larger target here is Thomas Mann's literary output. As George Steiner points out, the irreverence of this work brightens with laughter the monumental achievements of Mann's career.[4] The context here is the relation between Mann and his reading public. Near eighty when he took up the continuation of the Krull story, he was sufficiently disengaged from his own career to poke fun at earnestness. Thus Felix's style at times verges on a parody of Mann's own weighty attempts to make sense of the twentieth century. Irreverence is the right word—all solemnities dissolve when Felix gets his pen around them. The pretence that is literature can be fun. Mann concluded the volume in such a way that Felix could have pursued his adventures around the world, but there was no need for a sequel. Mann had made his final point.

This analysis of the literary complexities of Mann's foolery may seem to have ranged far from my central concern with the figure of the confidence man, but it has been necessary background to defining Felix's particular nature as a con man and hence Thomas Mann's contribution to the evolution of this character type. Conning appears on all layers of the narrative, including that of Felix as narrator and hence the ostensible creator of his confessions. As Mann remarked of Book One before he wrote the continuation, it is a portrait of the artist in which "the element of the unreal and illusional passes frankly over into the criminal."[5] In the text as a whole we are dealing with a "con artist" in both the literal and the figurative senses.

The artist and the con man share, in Mann's portrait, a symbiotic relationship with their clients. The three childhood influences Felix credits with inspiring his later life embody different facets of the artist's ability to improve on nature in order to satisfy human needs for fulfilment through fantasy. Felix's godfather, the hack painter Schimmelpreester, encourages Felix's childhood exploits in dressing up as anyone from the Kaiser to Hermes. His tutelary genius is Phidias, magnificent as sculptor and as thief, implying that the splendour of art is inseparable from the moral taint of fakery. Similarly Müller-Rosé, the actor, is ugly and pockmarked off stage but a magnificent hero in the eyes of the spectators who see him in a play. Müller-Rosé's name evokes wine as does *"Schimmelpreester"*, which is roughly equivalent to the French *vin de paille*, exceptionally rich vintage made from individually picked over-ripe grapes. Together these names imply that the heady effects of wine are analogous to the "improvements on nature" created by painters and actors. Wine emerges once again, this time bottled, in association with Felix's father, who makes his living selling a fanciful "champagne" called *Loreley extra cuvée*. Unfortunately the wine, despite the elaborate promises of its label, is so miserable that Engelbert Krull goes bankrupt and commits suicide. It proves an object lesson to Felix on how not to manipulate appearances. Rather than subject his fortunes to the sale of a physical product, he will traffic more safely in illusions, images, and fantasies.

The artist as con man retains his identifying relationship with his victims. Criminal con men fleece only those who have become co-conspirators. Similarly Felix Krull only services those whose need for fantasy or illusion leads them to assent to his offerings. He can then describe them not as victims but as partners or collaborators. Not unexpectedly Felix encounters a long succession of individuals who welcome his services to mankind. Genovefa, the family maid, is doomed by her poverty to abstinence or else lower-class lovers who would demean her status; therefore Felix serves her needs by allowing her to introduce him to sex. When he later fakes epileptic fits which entice an Army doctor into excusing him from military service, Felix can identify the doctor as his "partner" because the latter has co-operated so eagerly in order to show off his "superior" medical knowledge to his colleagues. From Felix's point of view as a con man, all parties are served by such collaboration; the world is admirably arranged.

In Felix's career at the St. James and Albany Hotel in Paris, higher ambitions emerge as his personal charm and skillful flattery make him irresistible to various guests, male and female. From then on he wants not simply to service others but to be accepted in the *beau monde* as an equal. This overriding urge seduces him, just once, into trying to impose his needs on another without her assent. This signal exception to the con man's proper relation to his victim deserves particular attention.

I have already remarked that on the narrative level which engages Felix as character with his successive "partners", many events are dominated by the logic of a "double image". The moral core of Felix's conmanhood resides here. The first introduction of the double image occurs in Chapter IV of Book Two when Felix, in his late teens, is passionately savouring the life of the rich as he sees it reflected in elegant shop windows and the wealthy crowds outside theatres. One afternoon a brother and sister step for a moment onto a balcony of a splendid hotel. Felix is transfixed by the vision: their youth and beauty, their magnificence of dress and bearing. He perceives them as Jewish or Latin, perhaps Spanish or Portuguese. The double image has sexual implications as well, though they are for the moment obscurely developed: *"Liebes-träume, Träume, die ich liebte, eben weil sie von—ich möchte sagen—ursprünglicher Ungetrenntheit und Unbestimmtheit, dop-pelten und das heisst doch erst: ganzen Sinnes waren, das berückend Menschliche in beiderlei Geschlechtsgestalt selig umfas-sten"* (65). ("Dreams of love, dreams that I loved precisely because —I firmly believe—they were of primal indivisibility and indeter-minateness, double; which really means that only then is there a significant whole blessedly embracing what is beguilingly human in both sexes" 77). The double image embodies both Felix's social ambition and his sense of partnership.[6] He dreams of joining them on the balcony above the rest of the world and as "Marquis Louis Venosta" he will succeed, though not precisely as he at first imag-ines. The sexual implications must first be sorted out.

The elaboration of the double image begins almost at once when Felix as Venosta boards a train for Lisbon on the first leg of his world tour. If the original Marquis had his beauteous mistress, Zaza, the newly christened Marquis wants her counterpart. Dining on the train, Felix-Louis meets the man who will ultimately pro-vide him with both partner and justification for joining her. Pro-fessor Kuckuck of the starry eyes (*"Sternenaugen"*, 203) possesses a detached and cosmic view of the universe and also a beautiful eighteen-year-old daughter named Zouzou. Felix will try to acquire both, though not without some difficulties.

Professor Kuckuck is the chief paleontologist of the Lisbon Natural History Museum. He welcomes Krull-Venosta to the city by offering him both his philosophy and the company of his wife and daughter. Felix delightedly accepts both and finds that they are considerable interrelations. In Zouzou he hopes to find his equivalent of Zaza and in Kuckuck's playful identification of Felix with the fossil animal the sea lily, the latter takes his cue for how to approach her. In adulthood the sea lily, which like Felix is

78

"entrail-less" (295; *"eingeweidelosen"*, 236), emancipates itself from its roots and sets off adventurously wandering the world. Since Felix indeed lives a foundationless existence (349), marriage with Zouzou is out of the question. Seduction is not.

Even for seduction Professor Kuckuck is helpful.[7] In his scientist's view all moral restraints are absurd since all bodies are mere combinations of cells, obedient to the impersonal and impartial laws of nature. Through geologic time nature has spontaneously evolved toward man as its highest creation, but even man's time is limited. All life began from Nothingness and will return in time to the primeval state. Among all the creatures man alone is conscious of the inevitability of both Beginning and End and his awareness that all life is but an episode in time shifts his values from the permanent to the transitory. Felix eagerly seizes these theories—in them his amoral, sea-lily life is justified.

The moral is clear: the sabre-toothed tiger and the giant armadillo lived for a time in symbiotic interdependence only to perish when conditions changed, so Felix must hasten to find his partner in the dance of life. No longer will he dance to the tune of Diane Houpflé or others. His earlier notion of himself as an artist serving the human need for fantasy has been dwarfed and swallowed up in the new cosmic perspective. It is now the principle of all existence he implements in setting about to seduce Zouzou. It remains to be seen, however, if that pairing will prove genuinely symbiotic.

Felix's attempts are distracted by the continual presence of Zouzou's mother to the extent that he explicitly links the two to his earlier double-image:

> *Ausdrücklich merkte ich an, dass dieses Entzücken mir von keiner der beiden Figuren für sich, weder von ihm noch von ihr allein hätte erregt werden können, sondern dass ihre Zweiheit, ihr holdes Geschwistertum es war, was es mir so antat. Den Menschenfreund wird es interessieren, wie diese Neigung zur Doppelbegeisterung, zur Bezauberung durch das Ungleich-Zweifache sich hier, statt am Geschwisterlichen, an der Mutter-Tochter-Beziehung bewährte.* (224–25)

I remarked explicitly that such excitement could not have been aroused in me by either of the figures alone, either his or hers, but that their lovely brother-and-sister duality was what moved me so deeply. The connoisseur of humanity will be interested in the way my penchant for twofold enthusiasms, for being enchanted by the double-but-dissimilar, was called into play in this case by mother-and-daughter instead of brother-and-sister. (281)

Since Donna Maria Pia is a formidable duenna, watchful and proudly Iberian, Felix concludes that his strategy must maintain at least the appearance of wooing both mother and daughter. He is rarely with one when the other is not present. If he pays a compliment to one and kisses her hand, his eyes are directed to the other. He engages in elaborate analyses of their differing claims to beauty. None the less this new double image presents some particular problems. The original brother-sister pairing combined both sexes with a yin-and-yang wholeness; the mother-daughter pair contains only one sex. For Felix himself to enter it, the image must be split; one of the ladies must step aside so that Felix can join the other.

Though mistakenly, Felix concentrates his efforts on Zouzou, still trying to complete the image of Venosta with his Zaza. He finds her not only pretty in body but pert in conversation and stubbornly moral in her evasion of his advances. Felix is distressed to encounter for the first time in his career someone with an apparently genuine moral sense, an innocent who admits no need for his "services". Felix musters all his charm, his skill at flattery, even the anti-moralistic arguments he has just learned from Professor Kuckuck, all to no avail. But Felix has forgotten his earlier con man's code that the victim must be co-operative and besides he has not yet learned all that Professor Kuckuck has to teach. The final lesson, this time about bullfighting, leads to Felix's union with the experienced mother rather than the innocent daughter, a pairing which preserves the code.

At the bullfight the professor's explanation of its primitive ritual helps Felix realize that his pursuit of Zouzou was out of tune with both his past life and the nature of the universe. The *corrida*, according to Kuckuck, preserves a primitive human rite, more blood-basic than Christianity and hence more profoundly "true".

Getauft worden seien die Neulinge ihres Glaubens nicht mit Wasser, sondern mit dem Blut eines Stieres, der vielleicht der Gott selber gewesen sei, wiewohl der auch wieder in dem gelebt habe, der sein Blut vergoss. Denn diese Lehre habe etwas unscheidbar Verkittendes, auf Tod und Leben Zusammenschmiedendes gehabt für alle ihr Angehörigen, und ihr Mysterium habe in der Gleichheit und Einheit bestanden von Töter und Getötetem, Axt und Opfer, Pfeil und Ziel. (297)

Its converts had been baptized not with water, but with the blood of a bull, who was perhaps the god himself, though the god lived too in the one who spilled his blood. For this teaching contained something that united its believers irrevocably, joining them in life and in death; and its mystery consisted in the equality and identity of slayer and slain, axe and victim, arrow and target. (373)

Such is the religion appropriate to the Professor's world-view: the crucial notion is the equality and identity of the slayer and the slain. In it is implicit the final sexual development of the double image and its justification of Felix's career as confidence man.

The confidence man, as we have seen, works by sharing guilt with his partner-victim. The same has been true for Felix up to the time he sets about trying to seduce Zouzou, the one stubbornly moral person he has encountered. In his eagerness to see himself finally installed on the balcony of high society, he tries to destroy her moral reserve. If Zouzou were to submit to him, she would be simply a victim and Felix a seducer. The basic principle of shared guilt which has justified his earlier activities would have been violated. The bullfight and its aftermath assure that he will abandon that false goal in favour of his appropriate union with her mother.

Maria Pia da Cruz Kuckuck, up to the time of the bullfight, has seemed to Felix a haughty strong beauty, possessed of an instinctive nobility he ascribes to ancient Iberian blood and a proud dignity appropriate to Zouzou's efficacious duenna. She seemed to Felix a woman whose behaviour was carefully controlled and principled, therefore unpromising as a partner for him. The bullfight reveals her deeply passionate nature through the heaving of her bosom, which Felix gratefully re-encounters in his final union with her and the primordial forces. She and not her innocent daughter is worthy to re-enact with him the primitive ritual of love-making in which exploiter and victim are indissolubly linked and indistinguishable.

81

Thus Felix finally takes his place in the double image, which has itself grown to encompass the fundamental principle of life. The same symbiotic interdependence the Professor pointed out between the armadillo and the saber-toothed tiger rules the moral world as well. The Professor himself is thus Felix's final tutelary spirit. With his lofty withdrawal beyond morality, the Professor could hardly object to his wife's infidelity with Felix. Instead he promulgates a worldview which projects the confidence man's amoral existence as the essence of the cosmos. Felix could not ask for a more inclusive justification for his life.

Of course, Mann's multiple justification of conmanhood is undercut from the beginning by the framing of the narrative. In a fictional world where all is acknowledged to be pretence, including fiction itself, nothing can seem too serious. Even Felix's tone as narrator is so solemn as to be humorous. Robert Heilman is right to associate the work with the picaresque mode in which the rogue cavorts on a holiday from serious restraints or weighty moral judgments.[8]

In this work, Mann undoubtedly had other things on his mind besides portraying the con artist at work and play. He was clearly fascinated by the mythological implications of Felix as Hermes, a dimension studied in detail by Donald Nelson.[9] But in the present context what matters most is Mann's domestication of the confidence figure. If Gide toyed with a perspective which decriminalized the con man, Mann has domesticated him, installed him in the master bedroom in the dual sense of emphasizing his ties with respectably hypocritical middle-class values and also featuring him in a pleasant play for puritans suitable for bedtime reading.

Felix's successor among these portraits is considerably more ominous. Not content with claiming moral equality with middling humanity, Camus' Jean-Baptiste Clamence installs himself in an imaginary courtroom where he will pass judgment on ordinary mortals. Instead of the lighthearted confessions of a con man, we will have the con man as confessor—in the double sense of the person who confesses and also expects to hear confessions.

NOTES

1. Citations are from the 1965 edition of A. Fischer Verlag: Frankfurt-am-Main, and from the Modern Library edition of Denver Lindley's translation which first appeared in 1955. Page references to these editions are identified in parentheses.

2. Mann finished and published Book One of the present three in 1911. His continuation is masterfully consistent, though Erich Heller and others exaggerate when they claim that not a word is changed in the later version of Book One. In particular Mann dropped the original name of Felix's godfather, "Maggotson" in favour of the more felicitous and wine-punning *"Schimmelpreester"* (see above, p. 76). See Heller's "Parody, Tragic and Comic: Mann's *Doctor Faustus* and *Felix Krull"*, *Sewanee Review* 64 (1958), 540.

3. The term and analytic technique are derived from Erving Goffman, *Frame Analysis: An Essay on the Organization of Experience* (Cambridge, Mass., 1974). This book is a stimulating contribution to social psychology, though it is vitiated by Goffman's tendency to lose the forest for the trees.

4. George Steiner, *Language and Silence* (New York, 1970), 270.

5. "Preface", *Stories of Three Decades*, trans. H. T. Lowe-Porter (New York, 1936), vii.

6. The importance of the double-image has been noted by many critics, though not, to my knowledge, interpreted in the present fashion. See, for example, Eva Schiffer, "Illusion und Wirklichkeit in Thomas Mann's *Felix Krull* und *Joseph"*, *Monatsheft* 55 (1962), 69–81, esp. 73–4.

7. My interpretation runs counter to those of commentators who find Professor Kuckuck's discourses only marginally relevant to the main stream of the action. See, for example, J. W. Smeed, "The Role of Professor Kuckuck in *Felix Krull"*, *Modern Language Review* 59 (1964), 411–12, or Donald B. Sands, "The Light and Shadow of Thomas Mann's *Felix Krull"*, *Renascence* 13 (1961), 119–24.

8. See "Variations on Picaresque (Felix Krull)", as reprinted in *Thomas Mann: A Collection of Critical Essays* ed. Henry Hatfield (Englewood Cliffs, N.J., 1964), 155–69.

9. *Portrait of the Artist as Hermes* (Chapel Hill, N. C., 1971).

5

Albert Camus and the Con Man as John the Baptist

> Money, you think, is the sole motive to pains and hazard, deception and deviltry, in this world. How much money did the devil make by gulling Eve?
>
> —Melville, *The Confidence Man*

Though Camus' *La Chute* (*The Fall*, 1956) was published only two years after Felix Krull's confessions, it moves to the other side of a major watershed dividing the works studied here. From here on the confidence men will no longer seek goals recognizably similar to those of their criminal prototypes. Their methods remain comparable to those of Felix Krull and his predecessors, thereby allowing us to recognize them as con men, but their goals shift from the criminal and social spheres to the moral and religious. Thus Camus' Clamence will present himself as the John the Baptist for a new clemency that offers release from oppressive feelings of personal guilt plus moral superiority over the rest of mankind—a pretty package though the price is high. Gone is the relative tangibility of Felix Krull's social goals. Gone is his implied claim to essential innocence because fakery is normal in both life and literature. Here the act of confession is no longer an excuse but a weapon.

The reader's relation to the confidence character also changes definitively with Clamence. Up to this point the reader has been placed essentially as an observer, even in the case of Felix Krull where the narration is first person. Felix's partner-victims, after all, are not heard from aside from his account of what went on. Still more important, we are invited to view his various encounters from the comfortable distance established by Krull-narrator. In Gide and Melville the reader is similarly an outsider looking on. Starting with Camus, the reader is tied above all to the victim, a reflection of the confidence figure's rise in status and esteem. The reader as representative of ordinary humanity can only be increasingly victimized by the confidence man as the latter claims ever higher stature and worth. Having been rehabilitated from moral stigma through Gide and Mann, he moves on toward his final claim of godhood.

In the case of Camus the narration is still a first-person mono-logue, but the reader is assimilated to Clamence's interlocutor, a shadowy listener whose words are never reported directly. At best the reader gathers that the listener, like Clamence, is fortyish, cul-tured, a man of the world. Even this sketchy description emerges in-directly through Clamence's attempts to categorize his listener in order to slant his confession more effectively. The reader is aware of the listener's continuing presence only insofar as Clamence infre-quently rephrases his remarks or weaves a response to them into his monologue. Thus the listener provides the occasion for Clam-ence's performance and the ostensible object of it, but he serves ultimately as a literary device for reducing the distance between the con man and the reader. If Clamence succeeds in trapping his victim, that victim will be the reader.

Our recognition of a con game at work depends on the way Clamence manipulates his listener-reader, a process which is complex both thematically and structurally. The core structures deserve attention first because they condition the intellectual en-trapment that Clamence hopes to complete by the end of the narrative. In *Felix Krull*, we recall, the essential structures are most easily conceived on a vertical axis as narrative levels are contained in and modified by progressively more inclusive narra-tive frames. Here the crucial axis is horizontal, the step-by-step succession of ideas through which Clamence leads his interlocutor, for Clamence is always in control, always ahead—in several senses. In particular, the thematic con is reiterated in a literary con that Clamence deftly practices on us when he reorients the status of the narrative near its end.

Clamence, like the Ancient Mariner, catches and holds his listener-reader by the impassioned recounting of his life story, in this case the confession of his duplicitous life as an upright and altruistic Paris lawyer. His promise is to explain how he arrived at his present profession as a "judge-penitent" practising in a sleazy bar on the Amsterdam waterfront. By the end of his account, however, he acknowledges that the "real" status of the story is to be itself part of the practice of judge-penitentship. That is, the promise to explain this curious profession is beginning to act it out. The narrative as a whole *is* what it purported to lead up to.

Failure to recognize this retroactive shift in narrative status has caused problems to critics. Wayne Booth, for example, is troubled by Clamence as an unreliable narrator because he admits that truth and falsehood are inextricably intertwined in his narrative.[1] Booth accepts the first level definition of the narrative as the story of Clamence's earlier life and hence he worries about the lack of verifiability in his account. But on the second-level redefinition of the narrative this problem disappears. Here Clamence, as he claims, is perfectly consistent: his entire presentation, viewed as the practice of judge-penitentship, works to drag the reader in his wake. As he says: *"Et mes histoires, vraies ou fausses, ne tendent-elles pas toutes à la même fin, n'ont-elles pas le même sens? Alors, qu'importe qu'elles soient vraies ou fausses si, dans les deux cas, elles sont significatives de ce que j'ai été et de ce que je suis"* (1535).[2] ("And whether my stories are true or false, don't they all point to the same end, don't they all have the same implication? So what difference does it make if they are true or false if in either case they signify what I was and what I am?") In short we are back in the world of Melville's Chapter XIV of *The Confidence Man* which shows that truth in the sense of verisimilitude is, for lack of evidence, irrelevant to literature. Clamence's literary trick has been to activate the listener-reader's expectation of a conventional realistic story while all the time practicing on him the tricks of judge-penitentship. This trickery on the level of narrative status correlates with what Clamence begins enforcing line by line as soon as he captures the listener's attention.

Before we can appreciate the full richness of the con game being played, we need to examine in detail just how Clamence maintains and extends his control over the listener-reader because here theme and structure are one. Precision here is the more important because unlike most confidence men in literature, Clamence is shown at work on only one victim. Camus does make it plain that his activity as judge-penitent is habitual, though each victim may call forth a different version of the pitch tailored specifically to his nature.

Clamence's success as a con man depends essentially on his ability to stage-manage his increasing intimacy with his victim, but there are certain factors basic to the situation which help him. The listener is a Frenchman, alone in a foreign city where he does not speak the language. He is subject to some of the same social temptations the con man in Robert Greene's London played on. Also, a person instinctively resistant to Clamence's blandishments would not likely wander into the Mexico City Bar in the first place. A singlemindedly moral and respectable individual like Felix Krull's Zouzou would never go there. Thus Clamence's victims help to select themselves when boredom or unhappiness lead them to his courtroom.

The limitation to a single encounter between con man and victim yields an unusually intense example of how the former operates. Clamence must maintain a measured control over the pace with which he unfolds his story. If he proceeds too rapidly, the listener may be frightened away from returning the following day. If he goes too slowly, both listener and reader may lose interest. The spinning of these confessions over five days is a dramatic achievement that could be appreciated by any extra-literary con man.

One example of careful engineering of intimacy must suffice. Through their five meetings Clamence moves through epithets of direct address that invoke increasing closeness. At first Clamence addresses his victim with the guardedly polite, *"monsieur et cher compatriote"*. The following evening he advances to *"cher monsieur"*. By the third encounter the listener is *"mon cher compatriote"*. Thereafter Clamence moves through *"cher ami"* to *"cher"*, *"mon cher"*, then to *"très cher"*. His final address is *"cher maître"*, implying a mock deference to the status of one whom he now knows to be a Paris lawyer like his own earlier self. These epithets signal Clamence's gradual presumption of community between the two.

To show the specifics of conning technique at work I want to

87

zero in on the first two pages of the narrative to demonstrate in detail the movement which is echoed later in Clamence's more abstract intellectual manipulations. The novel opens in the Mexico City Bar where the clientele falls into two groups. There are the steady customers, the whores, pimps, and thieves of Amsterdam whom Clamence serves as judge-advocate and then there are the visitors, tourists or perhaps middle-class Dutchmen slumming their way through the varied pleasures available on the waterfront. From among these Clamence selects those whom he offers to serve as judge-penitent. The novel opens with Clamance speaking to accost a stranger who seems to need help ordering from the grumpy bartender.

He begins his pitch by imposing in a touristic context the same sort of servile dominance he will gradually assert in the moral realm. He greets the listener as a newcomer to the Mexico City Bar who ostensibly needs help getting served. He offers to order genever gin from the barman, who speaks only Dutch. The reader cannot be perfectly sure that the listener in fact wanted Dutch gin, but Clamence in ordering it manages to imply that his intended victim would not be sure of being served at all if it were not for his benevolent intervention. The stranger finds himself already obligated to Clamence.

Invited to join his grateful victim, Clamence unleashes a dazzling swirl of ideas and observations that result in densely strategic prose from the outset. His first four paragraphs, which cover only two pages, can serve as a microcosm for the conning technique he will apply on a larger scale throughout his monologue. He leads the listener's attention through a swift succession of judgments from various points of view about the barman, himself, the Dutch, humanity in general. This rapid-fire shifting of perspective is both intriguing and bewildering but not, analysis shows, random.

Conceptually Clamence's method is most easily visualized as a rising spiral traced out by his successive positions as he shifts rapidly from one perspective to a higher one (see accompanying diagram). Note that Clamence himself, because his consciousness traces out the spiral motion, is at each moment higher than the events or people he looks down on—including himself at an earlier moment when he professed a "lower" point of view.

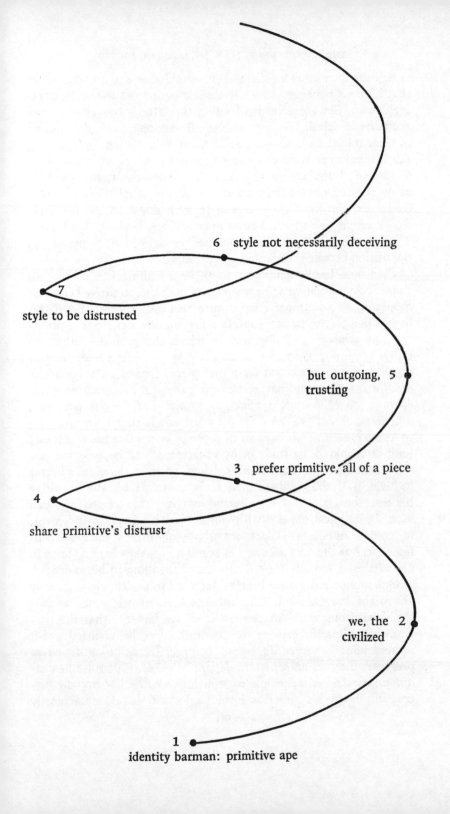

6 style not necessarily deceiving

7
style to be distrusted

but outgoing, 5
trusting

3 prefer primitive, all of a piece

4
share primitive's distrust

we, the 2
civilized

1
identity barman: primitive ape

Paragraph one, as we have seen, establishes the initial contact that allows Clamence to install himself beside the victim. In paragraph two, Clamence begins leading the latter's thoughts up and around the spiral. He begins, logically enough, with the ground of their initial meeting—the simian barman. Arbitrarily assigning the barman to position one at the base of the spiral, we can see how Clamence's initial comment places himself and the listener together at point two, a half-turn up and around the spiral. They are civilized men who have every reason to look down on the primitive Cro-Magnon type who has never mastered any language but Dutch. Thus the first loop of the spiral will be defined in terms of the opposition between cultivated and primitve.

Clamence hardly pauses a moment to allow the listener to share their mutual sense of superiority over the primitive before he moves up an additional quarter-turn to position three. From this higher perspective he can confess a certain nostalgia for the primitive, an awareness of one way in which the primitive might be more admirable than the civilized: *"Je vous l'avouerai, je suis attiré par ces créatures tout d'une pièce. Quand on a beaucoup medité sur l'homme, par métier ou par vocation, il arrive qu'on éprouve de la nostalgie pour les primates. Ils n'ont pas, eux, d'arrière-pensées"* (1475–76). ("I must admit that I am attracted by these creatures who are all of a piece. When one has meditated long on mankind, by trade or by vocation, it can happen that one feels nostalgia for the primates. They, at least, have no ulterior motives.") If the civilized man feels nostalgia for the primitive because the latter has no ulterior motives, then clearly civilized men, by implication, act with duplicity. This implicit judgment, of course, applies to Clamence above all others since he confesses it, but the very fact of his admission makes him, at least in his own eyes, morally superior to those unwilling to be so candid.

One more quarter-turn brings Clamence to position four directly above the barman with Clamence now siding with him against the duplicitous world of the civilized. He laments that the barman has himself been partly corrupted by the civilized babel around him: *"A force de ne pas comprendre ce qu'on dit en sa présence, il a pris un caractère défiant"* (1476). ("Because he cannot understand what people around him say, he has become distrustful.") On his superior level Clamence shares momentarily

the apeman's distrust of the civilized, but having come full circle
with one set of terms, he deftly transfers attention to himself and
shifts the relevant categories to trust and distrust.

Clamence affirms that he shares the barman's mistrust except
that (another half-turn up to position five) his outgoing nature
doesn't allow him to stop there: *"J'estime sa méfiance fondée et
la partagerais volontiers si, comme vous le voyez, ma nature com-
municative ne s'y opposait. Je suis bavard, hélas! et me lie facile-
ment. Bien que je sache garder les distances qui conviennent,
toutes les occasions me sont bonnes"* (1476). ("I judge his lack of
confidence to be justified and I would willingly share it except, as
you see, for my sociable nature. Alas, I talk a lot and get attached
easily. Though I know how to keep an approprate distance, every
sort of occasion is useful to me.") With the turning of the spiral
Clamence at position five is directly above the point at which he
initially affirmed the obvious superiority of his civilized listener
and himself over the primitive barman. By now proclaiming his
own trustfulness, Clamence in effect reasserts, at position five,
his common bond with the cultivated listener. He goes on to call
attention to his own cultivation by using the imperfect subjunctive.
This uncommon tense will serve as the basis for his next turn
around the spiral.

In contemporary French the imperfect subjunctive is considered
too literary and refined for conversational use. Showing off his
mastery of this stylistic elegance accomplishes two purposes for
Clamence. First he confirms from his companion's knowing response that both men share a similar educational background.
Still more important the notion of style provides the terminology
for looking back down on civilization once again from the higher
perspectives of positions six and seven. Position six, a quarter-turn
beyond trust in cultivation, represents a reluctant and partial
apology for elegant appearances: he acknowledges that a taste for
fine linen does not necessarily imply that one's body is dirty. But
his next thought in effect carries him further to position seven
where the barman's and his own earlier distrust of appearances is
reiterated: style, like filmy clothing, often conceals a nasty skin
condition.

Clamence closes this sequence of spiralling with a blanket judgment that he will restate and reimpose with increasing force and

91

explicitness throughout his monologue. If his discourse is directed with malicious intent, those whose thoughts meander are not pure either. Herein lies the core of his manipulative method. He condemns himself—though so far for the relatively benign fault of excessive love of style and elegance—and he has affirmed that all civilized appearances are untrustworthy, that everyone suffers from doubleness, even the simian barman. Therefore everyone is guilty of false pretences.

If all are by implication equally impure, Clamence none the less maintains a measure of superiority as the one who enunciates that judgment in the process of controlling the movement of perspectives that leads to it. He sees around the next turn up the spiral and leads the listener's consciousness through progressive stages of looking back down on the previous position in order to condemn it.

As Clamence's monologue unfolds, spiralling is less explicitly evident in his step-by-step leading of the listener-reader, though it still controls the larger movement of his intrigue. The larger spiral turns around an unending succession of confessions and self-condemnations. In graphic detail Clamence recounts his earlier life as a Paris lawyer who leapt to defend murderers, widows and orphans, to manipulate judges with elegant discourses on innocence and justice. He reinforced his unflappably good opinion of himself by means of the easy submission of women to his whims. But this Edenic period of contentment with himself and certainty of moral superiority over others came to an end. His own guilty conscience could no longer let him stay unaware of his hypocrisy and duplicity. His response then, he says, was to recognize that innocence is merely lack of self-awareness. As he now confesses to his listener-reader, Clamence looks back and down on his socially correct actions. He affirms that he is now superior not only to his former self but to all those who maintain a good opinion of themselves while leading a life based on common social masks and pretentions, the interlocutor and the reader presumably among them. Clamence is setting the stage for inviting us to follow him up the spiral by means of comparable confession and self-condemnation.

At every point the listener finds himself inferior to Clamence, in candor if not in self-insight. The latter, after all is leading the

game, and by the third encounter he is even ready to hint implicitly at a pending confession which would expose his earlier
confessions as themselves fabricated. He sketches a vision of hell
as the place where all humankind will wear a single unchanging
label forever. His own symbol in such a hell would be a charming
Janus face; his motto *"Ne vous y fiez pas"*, i.e. "Don't trust it";
his profession *comédien*, play-actor (1498). This set of labels invites the listener to ponder the present interchange as part of the
game and forces him to place his trust somewhere in relation to
Clamence. If he distrusts Clamence's recital of his earlier life,
he will have trusted the label, "No trust". If he distrusts the label,
then he will have trusted Clamence's account. In such a logical
bind, we are moving back toward a Melvillean world of unre-
solvable ambiguity. Whichever alternative he chooses, the listener-
reader seems entangled in looking up to Clamence as he pirouettes
up the spiral of self-condemnation. In the process the Janus face
becomes equivocal on both sides; the "real" Clamence, by his own
acknowledgement, is not knowable.

The moral fog Clamence is generating appears physically in their
fourth meeting. The Zuyderzee provides its habitual fog to accom-
pany a ferry boat ride during which he continues to collapse traditional moral dualities like innocence-guilt and trust-distrust into
the grey soup of duplicity. Clamence's key metaphor here is the
"little-ease", a medieval torture cell recently reactivated in Viet-
nam as the tiger-cage. Just as the prisoner can neither stand nor
lie, he learns to feel his guilt because innocence, which would consist in being able to stretch, is impossible. The listener demurs,
apparently asserting that one might be imprisoned unjustly, but
Clamence insists that guilt unites all in abasement.

This premise is essential to Clamence's pitch because once it is
accepted, he who condemns himself first thereby gains moral
superiority through the virtue imputed to confession. The superior
"honesty" of self-condemnation restores the superiority he felt
when he thought himself innocent, once one further escape hatch
has been closed off—the possibility of redemption. Hence Clamence proceeds to discredit two Christian figures for redemption:
Jesus Christ and the Pope. The sinless innocence of Jesus disappears when Clamence interprets the cross as, in effect, a "little-
ease" chosen by Jesus because he himself acknowledged guilt,

however indirect, for the massacre of the innocents at Bethlehem.

The Pope retains Clamence's attention longer, as if he took that symbolic figure to be more of a threat to his system. In his final seance, held in the intimacy of his room, Clamence recounts a time during World War Two in North Africa when he was elected "pope" and moral judge over his fellows. The overtones here are far more serious than the playful anti-Pope played by Gide's Protos. The Germans have collected a motley group of prisoners in a desert camp. The men, tortured by thirst, find themselves in a modern "little-ease" that demonstrates their guilt. Clamence is elevated to his post of moral judge because he confesses to having more faults than anyone else. Hence he judges their relative merits, inevitably placing himself above them in other ways as well. He appropriates for himself the water due to a dying comrade on the grounds that the group needs his services as pope more than those of a mere follower. In addition to intensifying his confessions—the more awful the crime, the more laudable its confession—this story justifies Clamence's devaluing the real Pope. Having experienced in parody the temptations of moral authority, he can claim to pity the Pope, hence feel himself superior. By pardoning the Pope, Clamence elevates himself to higher status, in his own eyes at least.

With redemption safely out of the question, Clamence feels fully in command of the logic of his system and hence of the con he is trying to put on his listener-reader. A confidence man, we remember, cheats those who themselves falsify appearances in order to swindle others. He proceeds by offering a small-scale trial of the swindling scheme as a "convincer". The game is incomplete here because Camus carefully avoids defining the listener's response for very good reasons I will go into shortly, but the proffered bait is clear as well as the currency of gain he proposes. When guilt is universal and innocence an illusion, then the sole means to differentiate oneself from the mass of the guilty is confession of that guilt. Clamence has shown the way by castigating his own earlier life and from the mid-point on begins more and more insistently to invite comparable admissions by his listener. The prize would be the perpetuation of the listener-reader's sense of moral superiority despite the loss of innocence. The con would be that no matter how far he might go in confessing faults, Jean-Baptiste Clamence would be still further above him, having confessed first and furthest, leading back up a spiral of infinite regress.

At several places along the way Clamence has admitted his love of domination. He has always preferred mountain peaks to valleys, the upper decks of ships to cabins. Islands, in particular mountainous Sicily, are preferable because they are easier to dominate. He has a horror of speleologists or anyone who accepts narrow restraint. If his guilty conscience put him into a "little-ease", his con trick will spirit him up and out. He needs a victim so that he can have a follower to confirm his superiority without the possibility of catching up on the spiral of confession. *"C'est à qui crachera le premier, voilà tout"* (1530). ("He who spits first wins, that's all there is to it.")

In the final climactic encounter, these diverse movements of theme and structure converge and reveal their essential homology. Clamence transforms the status of the narrative in revealing that he has been practicing judge-penitentship all along. He can even go so far as to put himself above confessions as a genre by confessing yet once again. *"Les auteurs de confession écrivent surtout pour ne pas se confesser, pour ne rien dire de ce qu'ils savent. Quand ils prétendent passer aux aveux, c'est le moment de se méfier, on va maquiller le cadavre. Croyez-moi, je suis orfèvre"* (1536). ("The writers of confessions do so above all to avoid confessing, to say nothing of what they really know. When they pretend to tell all, that is the moment to distrust them: they're going to cover up the truth. Believe me, I am a pro at it.") Thus Clamence shows himself so confident that he can thoroughly blow the cover on his earlier manipulations. Since Clamence confesses his tendentiousness, the listener-reader is invited, once again, to "trust" him; the process could be extended *ad infinitum*.

Everything he has said, as Clamence finally admits openly, has been carefully directed to signify and to apply judge-penitentship. Jean-Baptiste Clamence continues to love himself and to make use of others (1546), just as he did more naïvely during his halcyon days in Paris. His control extends even to the ill health of which he has complained as early as the third encounter, but which "forces" him to receive the listener-reader in bed at the last. It allows him to exact minor personal services from the listener which serve as figure for the moral servitude he craves. In addition he manages to involve the listener in criminal guilt which figures the moral burden Clamence wants him to share. Clamence is concealing in his room a master painting, "The Just Judges", stolen years earlier from the Ghent Cathedral. By making the listener an accomplice after the fact, Clamence has literally loaded guilt on him. Even if the listener should turn him in to the police, Clamence can envision a triumph with his severed head held up above the mob, the culmination of a career as false prophet who clamours (the second-stage echo in his name) in the desert. Thus Clamence closes as he opened, condemning himself from further and further up the spiral that continues as long as he.

Clamence poses thereby the unexpected problem of the "honest" con man who acknowledges what he is doing in the very act of continuing his pitch. Confessing the conscious attempt to manipulate the listener-reader lays claim to still higher appreciation of his honesty. Thus Clamence carries out the logic of his confessional to the extent of exposing the method itself as a further extension of its application.

Now it takes a confident confidence man to risk exposing his method. Clamence is willing to do so because he feels sure that he has analysed to an inescapable conclusion the situation of mankind in the modern world. No matter how cautious the listener may be, Clamence believes he can afford to wait: *"Oui, vous êtes un client difficile. . . . La plupart des autres sont plus sentimentaux qu'intelligents; on les désoriente tout de suite. Les intelligents, il faut y mettre le temps. Il suffit de leur expliquer la méthode à fond. Ils ne l'oublient pas, ils réfléchissent. Un jour ou l'autre, moitié par jeu, moitié par désarroi, ils se mettent à table"* (1546). ("Yes, you're a difficult customer. . . . Most of the others are more emotional than intelligent; one puts them off balance right away. For intelligent ones one has to put in a lot of time. It is sufficient to explain to them the method in depth. They don't forget, they reflect on it. One day or another, half playfully, half desperately, they sit down to sup.") Whether Clamence's confidence is justified or not, Camus wisely avoids clarifying.[3] If Clamence were to achieve a clear victory or suffer a clear defeat, the novel would close in on its own world instead of opening out into the reader's own reflections on himself and his world. Clamence, after all, true to the nature of the confidence man, has only such authority as the listener or reader assent to.

The listener-reader's response to Clamence's pitch remains, of course, his own, but the number of options are limited and will repay some consideration. Clamence operates within a partially post-Christian world. Neither he nor his interlocutor believe that the doves of grace will descend to re-establish innocence. Camus himself, in proposing a working title borrowed from Lermontov, "A Hero of Our Time", evidently conceived the work as encapsulating the experience of a generation which could feel guilt but no longer find redemption credible. Clamence, in any case, explicitly rules out redemption, leaving a hollow shell of Christian conceptions: guilt plus confession without absolution. The reader, as he moves out of the fiction back into his own world, may respond to Clamence's world view in one of three ways.

The first, perhaps least likely, is that he is convinced by Clamence's self-serving demonstration. In such a case the reader would logically become a convert to Clamenceism and go about preaching the life and ideas of that John the Baptist. A second possibility is that the reader locates his certainties in beliefs culturally prior to Clamence's—in traditional Christianity itself. Such a reader might well have found the whole game preposterous early on, once it became clear that Clamence denies the possibility of redemption. The third option responds to the situation of Camus, who created the work out of an agonized reappraisal of his own earlier values. The work grows out of and is addressed most directly to those for whom the shreds of Christianity can no longer be sewn together into a fabric sufficient to cover their nakedness. This third class of readers will most probably feel appalled at the horrors Clamence can perpetrate on the basis of his desperate half-Christianity. The long-term effect on such readers is likely to be a further distancing of themselves from the Christian presumptions remaining with them. Such is the common impact of confidence men within literature and without: the values they play upon to perform the con game, whether economic or social or moral, are devalued and discredited for those who are aware of or subject to the trickery. In this sense and for this type of reader, Camus' portrait of a confidence man at work can only hasten the cultural shedding of Christian values.

It is possible to read this novel without reference to the confidence man, but there are advantages to doing so, both internal and external. Internally the isolation of this pattern for inspection underlines the subtlety and maliciousness of Clamence's whole presentation. Seen beside those of his fellow con men, his motives become clear. Externally Clamence is a dazzling example of how at home a con man can seem in our time. That all men are masked fakers in their daily lives is a notion that comes early in his confession and low on his scale of guilt. Clamence hardly expects resistance on this point. If Clamence carries this notion out to a tortured extreme, as a self-appointed judge of mankind, it is still progressively easier as we approach our own time to conceive every man as a con man. Jean-Baptiste prepares the way for our next flowering of the con man in Kurt Vonnegut's Bokonon, the founder of a new religion for our time. In him the confidence figure becomes elevated above mankind as prophet and law-giver, a position to which Clamence could only aspire.

NOTES

1. See *The Rhetoric of Fiction* (Chicago, 1961), esp. 294–97.
2. The text of *La Chute* referred to is in *Théâtre, Récits, Nouvelles*, ed. Roger Quilliot (Paris, 1965), 1473–549. All references to this text are identified by page numbers in parentheses. English translations are mine.
3. W. Allen Whartenby in "The Interlocutor in *La Chute*: A Key to its Meaning", *PMLA*, 83 (October 1968), 1326–333, concludes that the listener has successfully resisted Clamence's blandishments. While the listener has certainly escaped as far as the text reports, Clamence seems satisfied with his confidence in future submission as quoted here. The question remains moot for the reader, an openendedness essential to Camus' engagement of his reader's moral reflections.

6

Kurt Vonnegut and the Con Man as Messiah

> Life is a pic-nic *en costume*; one must take a part, assume a character, stand ready in a sensible way to play the fool.
> —Melville, *The Confidence Man*

By this point in the proceedings I have examined enough specific portraits to encourage a retrospective glance over the several interrelated movements that their sequence allows. Two are most important. On the one hand, there is a distinct progression in the ground of engagement through which the reader perceives the confidence figure. On the other, there is a related movement of upward revaluation of the notion "confidence man" which is replete with implications of cultural evolution. These two are intimately linked because as the confidence figure loses his demonic association to become more secular, familiar, even domesticated, the grounds of his appeal to a reader shift correspondingly. Thus the first three of these portraits, which step-by-step raise the con man to "normal" human stature, orient the reader as an observer who is progressively more intimate with the con man himself. Melville seems ready enough to condemn the confidence figure if only he could grasp a reality sufficiently solid to allow clear identification of who is conning whom. Lacking such certainty, Melville's narrator keeps the reader a puzzled onlooker. Gide's narrator uses his omniscience to take the reader at least partway behind the scenes of the con man's life. Decriminalization results since once he is known from within the con man seems no more reprehensible than his respectable counterparts. In Mann we are fully behind the con man's eyes as Krull shapes his own story with an eye to winning our approval. Through exposing fakery at all levels of society and citing the scientific authority of Professor Kuckuck, Felix not surprisingly finds his life—and his telling of it—quite admirable after all.

If these first three portraits resuscitate the con man's reputation, the second three elevate him above mere human status toward godhood. In these instances the reader is progressively oriented to the victim. Camus is of capital importance here in preparing the way for Vonnegut's and Fowles' more recent portraits; his use of first-person narration, unlike Mann's, focuses the reader's awareness through the shadowy listener. At the same time the con man claims, even if the listener and reader resist, superior moral status. Vonnegut carries this process further when his narrator, after stout resistance, becomes a willing convert and hence victim of a con man who announces in advance that his religion is bogus. Note that what he offers is none the less a religion; the con man has attained, not merely claimed, moral superiority—given a rather special definition of the world.

After the high literary finesse of the authors treated so far Vonnegut's slapdash style and hodge-podge structure inevitably seem thin. I will wager that in fifty years or less he will be read as a minor figure representing a certain stage in the cultural decay of the West. Yet this latter factor is one of the reasons his confidence man earns a place in this portrait gallery. Besides helping in their limited ways to undermine and discredit traditional Western values, these confidence men also serve as sensitive barometers of the cultural weather—ever more stormy and obscure as far as inherited certainties are concerned. *Cat's Cradle* (1963) is an argument for the impossibility of maintaining credence in Christianity or its fosterchild, liberal humanism. The insanity of its fictional world is arranged to demonstrate their untenableness. Their values are exposed as fictions which can in turn become the subject of a fiction through the parodic religion offered by the confidence man Bokonon. As Glenn Meeter puts it, "Vonnegut rejects both Western religion, with its insistence on God's acts in history, and the novel, the Western art form which more than any other finds meaning in history."[1]

A moment of rudimentary theorizing may help to define the particular fictionality of this fiction. From an empirical point of view all fictions are lies. A higher order of fictiveness enters when a fiction centres on a confidence man who in advance labels all his statements as false. A reader knows full well when he picks up a novel that he will encounter fictions; if he didn't choose to do so, he would not open the book. Hence no reader will be put off by the first part of Vonnegut's epigraph: "Nothing in this book is true." By provisionally accepting the fictional world before him as "real", the reader is accustomed to encountering a reshaped version of the extra-fictional world he inhabits. When the central character he encounters on these expectations is an acknowledged fabricator himself, the reader is engaged in another order of construct, a fiction about fictions as they may appear in literature and outside literature. Fictions about fictions, like *Cat's Cradle*, abandon realistic probabilities in favour of internal consistency. Their relevance to the extra-literary world depends on each reader's attitude toward the fictions or fantasies that play a part in his everyday world. *Cat's Cradle* is a fiction which dramatizes one possible response to the end of the world for readers who inhabit a world which, however tenuously, continues to exist. The "meaning" of *Cat's Cradle* must be sought not in its suggestions about how to confront the end of the world, but in its weighing the consequences of falsehoods coming to seem more sensible than truths.

Vonnegut's novel depicts an absurd and hopeless world in which the only coherence is supplied artificially by a confidence man. It systematically excludes the notion of probability within itself. Bokonon denies that chance exists; whatever happens was *meant* to happen. A moment's reflection reminds us that when chance disappears, so does its reciprocal concept, probability. A chance even can be understood as one with immeasurably low probability. A fiction constructed without concern for probability will welcome and weave into its texture the unexpected in events, language, allusions and the like. The only test for relevance and appropriateness will be some measure of internal consistency.

The opposition of probability and consistency in this sense was first elaborated by Melville because the confidence man as character posed such a problem to his fellow characters and to the reader. Since he could find no basis for defining any probabilities as reliable, Melville was reduced to internal consistency as a measure for "truth". Clamence works the same vein when he says that it does not matter if his confessions are true or false because they all tend toward the same end. But if Clamence's aim is moral seduction, Bokonon's is to mock all possibilities of moral judgment. Hence he goes further by not only acknowledging his falsification as such but also by abandoning seriousness and consistency. His only consistent position is that everything he says is rubbish. The question is no longer what is trustworthy, but whether the victim can avoid, given the definition of the world he inhabits, placing trust in notions he knows to be false. The fictional world as a whole has been given over to the spirit of the confidence man who is beyond morality. All is playful invention, fabrication.

To say that *Cat's Cradle* is a fiction which internally justifies its non-realistic character amounts to more than a restatement of its links to science fiction. More important in the present context is the new relation it establishes between the reader and the core notion of a confidence man. All the other portraits sketched here since Melville presumed that there existed a world in which characters or by extension the reader had a choice about the extent to which they would play along with the con man. Vonnegut structures a world in which it seems impossible to avoid placing one's confidence in acknowledged put-ons. But at the same time the ominous associations of the confidence figure in earlier fictions diminish greatly. Once the universe seems inescapably absurd, the fabricator appears more refreshing than wicked. By acknowledging his lies, he allows them to be taken more lightly, as fictions within a fiction that are playful enough to be enjoyable for their own sakes.

Bokonon himself remarks that maturity is "a bitter disappointment for which no remedy exists, unless laughter can be said to remedy anything."[2] Laughter of course can at least offer some consolation and the humour that enriches *Cat's Cradle* is an essential part of its portrait of a world given over to the confidence spirit. The multiple disjunctures, wacky coincidences, incongruous allusions, jumbled levels of style, all contribute to a humorous acceptance of the human condition that is more lighthearted than grim. The structural mould of the novel itself is illustrative. The end of the world in all of its seriousness is elaborated through one hundred and twenty-seven chapters, each a blurt about a page long or less. The reader even has a cue to the offhandedness to come in the Table of Contents where the chapter titles are spread across the pages in unexpected patterns guided by irregular right-hand margins. The chapter titles themselves are a hodge-podge without cumulative sense. Richard Giannone points out that American editions of *Cat's Cradle* whimsically mock the reader's expectation of continuity and coherence by printing the mathematical symbol for therefore (∴) at the beginning of each chapter.[3]

The Books of Bokonon share such humorous incongruities with *Cat's Cradle. The Fourteenth Book,* for example, has the following discursive title: "What Can a Thoughtful Man Hope for Mankind on Earth, Given the Experience of the Past Million Years?" Its contents consist of one word and a period: "Nothing" (199). Similarly Bokonon's replacements for the psalms, the *Calypsos,* use doggerel to undercut any solemnity of sentiment. Some such deflating device is activated at every moment the narrator momentarily endorses a hopeful notion. The result in each case is a come-down to the hopelessness appropriate to a Bokononist. In Bokonon's world invitations to smile and to cry meet head-to-foot, like wave and undertow.

The playfulness permeating Vonnegut's literary technique conditions the reader's sense of the issues at stake. Despite and even partly because of the narrator's straight-faced earnestness, the characters he describes seem involved in nothing so much as an elaborate child's game. Such games are inherently non-utilitarian and literally inconsequential. As the novel draws to a conclusion, even Bokononism is reduced to child's play. *Ice-nine,* by depriving the world of a future, thereby eliminates the ostensible utility of the religion as a social and psychic pacifier. All activities become essentially pointless, to be carried on for whatever amusement they can yield. In case the reader, or writer, harbours any lingering pretention that literature accomplishes anything in the world, Vonnegut formally writes out the possibility of any audience for the work. Since the world is frozen stiff, who could edit, print, and distribute *Cat's Cradle?* It too is reduced to the level of the child's game which provides its title.

As a title "Cat's Cradle" is brilliantly chosen because its aura of childish amusement permeates the texture as a whole. The string game enters the novel through the recollections of the mid-

103

get Newt Hoenikker as he recalls the one time his atomic physicist father ever made any attempt to play with him. The day was 6 August 1945; Newt was six and the atom bomb was falling on Hiroshima. Felix Hoenikker, fiddling with a piece of string, responds to a sudden urge to use a cat's cradle for making contact with his son. As he bends down in the time-honoured ritual to invite the boy to "see the cat, see the cradle", in the webbing of string, Newt finds his father a perfect demon, face marked by gigantic pores, ears and nostrils stuffed with hairs, mouth breathing stale cigar smoke worthy of Hell itself. Newt flees in terror. He retains the label "cat's cradle" for all of the hopeful and traditional vacuities, like love and religion, that are passed on from one generation to the next.

The game "cat's cradle", then, exposes the fictions that traditionally keep civilization going. There never was a cat or a cradle, only an agreement foisted on the young by the old to maintain the fiction and to exact loyalty from all concerned. No wonder Vonnegut's most enthusiastic readers are under thirty, if not, twenty. From a Bokononist point of view all mythologies, creeds, nations, organizations and like groupings are similarly based on air. Bokononism itself will improve on its shoddy conventional predecessors by announcing from the beginning that it is nothing but a series of fictions. Thus the phoney solemnity attached to conventional values can be eliminated because Bokononism will not take itself seriously. Little Newt, for example, is a sound Bokononist except that he lacks its essential playfulness. He recognizes the meaninglessness of it all, but has not yet learned to draw a compensating pleasure from playing his own game, whether it be constructing a religion or a novel or whatever. Newt's oil paintings are only black without the mitigation of humour. In the best of Bokononist worlds every build-up earns its come-down, but if nothing can remain holy, on the other hand, the depths are not abysmal. After all, they provide the occasion for the consoling fictions to be constructed.

Of all the values of Christianity, only a peripheral one survives in Bokononism: belief in the importance of human feelings of well-being. The superstructure of the religion, its wacky theology and parodic rituals, is fabricated precisely to preserve good feelings against the incursions of life. The island of San Lorenzo through

104

five centuries of occupation and attempted exploitation by all the major colonial powers, including the Catholic Church and a U.S. sugar company, has proved stubbornly unimprovable. Life there is irretrievably Hobbesian: solitary, poor, nasty, brutish, and short. Since no real improvement is possible, the most sane and humane course, according to Bokonon, is to create a dramatic context which can take the minds of its citizens off their very tangible misery.

Bokononism offers the San Lorenzans a reassuringly simple view of the world, a down-to-earth Manicheanism as old as Zoroaster. Evil is located in the civil authority, currently headed by "Papa" Monzano, which outlaws the Good, represented by Bokonon himself. As soon as Bokonon, on his suggestion, is exiled to the jungle, his value, predictably, increases in the eyes of the people. In time everyone on the island becomes a practitioner of Bokononism while publicly denouncing it. Here is a religion that succeeds as an opiate for the people because it distracts their minds from the genuine and unchangeable misery Vonnegut posits for their lives. Their morale improves proportionately as they ingest the bogus morality: " 'But people didn't have to pay as much attention to the awful truth. As the living legend of the cruel tyrant in the city and the gentle holy man in the jungle grew, so, too, did the happiness of the people grow. They were all employed full time as actors in a play they understood, that any human being anywhere could understand and applaud' " (144). Herein lies the justification offered for Bokonon's fabrications. Of course the religion is phoney, but it benevolently shapes a world more pleasant for humans to inhabit.

Though Bokonon may seem a zany but essentially benevolent manipulator of mankind, he himself professes to no illusions about his essential character. He recognizes that he appears saintly only in the context of the religious drama which he himself has manufactured. He maintains that his advice is too worthless to follow, though others may follow it to the death, and he acts consistently with his self-deflation. But if the only value sacred to Bokonon is the human feeling of well-being, moral problems become problems of morale. If it takes lies to maintain morale, Bokonon will supply them complete with ironic self-devaluation.

If *Cat's Cradle* went no further than outlining Bokonon's well-meaning fakery on San Lorenzo, we might be enticed into the self-

105

cancelling judgment that he is the first genuinely benevolent con man. As it is, however, the novel imports into San Lorenzo a number of people and products of the larger world of the contemporary West which ultimately make the question senseless. In narrative terms these imports freeze the world to death and in parallel thematic terms, they result in a paralysis of the moral faculties which are necessary even to entertain such questions. *Cat's Cradle* affirms that Bokonon is a spiritual mountebank yet simultaneously immobilizes any moral context in which such fakery could be condemned.

The moral core of the novel is neatly symbolized in a figure who is mentioned only once: Charles Atlas, "mail-order musclebuilder", one of whose alumni is Bokonon himself. Bokonon has adapted from Atlas his chief advertising slogan: "Dynamic Tension" and turned it to his own uses.

> It was the belief of Charles Atlas that muscles could be built without bar bells or spring exercisers, could be built by simply pitting one set of muscles against another.
>
> It was the belief of Bokonon that good societies could be built only by pitting good against evil, and by keeping the tension between the two high at all times. (90)

To reconstruct Bokonon's "logic", it helps to conjure up the image of Charles Atlas as his torso decorated thousands of comic books and other magazines destined for young American males from the late 1920s on. His swelling musculature of arm and shoulder result from the simple tension between hands as they strain against each other. In theory, Charles Atlas need never move to build those muscles; maintaining the counterbalancing tension will do. As Tony Tanner rightly points out, a comparable tension is implicit in the game of Cat's Cradle: without it there would only be a muddle of string.[4]

The indecorous movement from the tawdry context of Charles Atlas to the ostensibly serious world of moral categories is a central element in Vonnegut's fictional technique. For the moment, however, the philosophical implications of "Dynamic Tension" are more important. "Good" and "Evil" are fictions to be flexed against each other to a stand-off. The resulting immobility has the effect of moral paralysis. Good and evil are no longer categories necessary for defining a moral shape to the world, but simply instinctive human reflexes which need to be neutralized by reciprocal tension. The narrative of *Cat's Cradle* proceeds through its journalist narrator to dramatize the inevitability of freezing the moral faculties into immobility, given the terminal limits Vonnegut ascribes to his fictional world.

The composition of *Cat's Cradle* ostensibly takes place after the world-freeze has given the narrator a final conversion to Bokononism. Thus he speaks from the retrospective point of view of the new convert who can see how gentle hints and pushes prepared the way. Virtually all the characters the narrator encounters on San Lorenzo help him along the road by confusing his ability to maintain clear distinctions between good and bad. Julian Castle, for example, is the offspring of the Castle Sugar family that exploited the island with small success from 1916 to 1922. When the narrator meets him, Julian has returned to San Lorenzo as its local Albert Schweitzer, offering the natives medicine and consolation to the extent possible. Prepared by his humanism to revere Castle, the narrator is taken aback to find him talking out of one side of his mouth like a Hollywood gangster. Before his selfless return to San Lorenzo he was best known for "lechery, alcoholism, reckless driving, and draft evasion. He had had a dazzling talent for spending millions without increasing mankind's stores of anything but chagrin" (76). The blend of decadence and good deeds is more than flabby humanism can cope with.

A comparable duality invades the narrator's emotions in the form by a sublimely oxymoronic woman, a blond negress named Mona Aamons Monzano, adopted daughter of "Papa" Monzano. The narrator falls in love even with her newspaper portrait and locates in her all the sexual and emotional fantasies engendered by two broken marriages and a foot-loose though well meaning life. Mona, it turns out, has a positive hostility to monogamous love and to those activities which produce babies. She is a thorough-going Bokononist, raised and tutored by the Messiah himself.

The loosing of *ice-nine* on the world was, from the narrator's original point of view, an accident that no human forethought could have predicted or prevented. For a Bokononist, however, there is no such thing as an accident. All things are ordained by

God, though their springs and motives are safely ensconced in incomprehensibility to humans. Or as *The Books of Bokonon* have it:

> Tiger got to hunt,
> Bird got to fly;
> Man got to sit and wonder, "why, why, why?"
> Tiger got to sleep,
> Bird got to land;
> Man got to tell himself he understand.
>
> (150)

When the narrator contemplates the odds on the world's survival once deadly devices are discovered by science and put into the hands of "fog-bound" children, he finds himself agreeing that whatever happens was *meant* to happen. Another step toward Bokononism, though the narrator resists to the end.

Even after the "grand ah-whoom" of *ice-nine* freezing and the days of tornadoes that follow, the narrator clings sentimentally to the shreds of his earlier humanism. He lauds Julian Castle for choosing to die in the tornadoes *en route* to his House of Mercy and Hope in the Jungle to offer what succour he can. He could do nothing of course and in his own Bokononist terms might as well be dead. The narrator insists on seeing such a death in terms of noble self-sacrifice for the sake of humanity. A lump rises in his throat as well when he thinks of Angela Hoenikker who picked up her clarinet from the frozen ruins to play her sorrowfully rich jazz without thinking about whether or not the mouthpiece might be contaminated with *ice-nine*. " 'Soft pipes, play on,' " he muses, mistily invoking Keats. The Bokononist come-down emerges from the mouth of the midget Newt: "Maybe you can find some neat way to die, too" (230).

His final conversion takes place in two stages. The first is his acceptance of the notion that he should find "a neat way to die, too". He wants to climb to the highest point on the island and die there with an appropriately symbolic gesture. The second stage is his first and final meeting with Bokonon, who will define the appropriate gesture and simultaneously conclude *Cat's Cradle*:

> If I were a younger man, I would write a history of human stupidity; and I would climb to the top of Mount McCabe and

lie down on my back with my history for a pillow; and I would
take from the ground some of the blue-white poison that makes
statues of men; and I would make a statue of myself, lying on
my back, grinning horribly, and thumbing my nose at You Know
Who.   (231)

Such a history, clearly, is *Cat's Cradle* and in this conclusion is
implicit the narrator's acknowledgement that Bokonon has the
last word.

This final Bokononist gesture confronting the end of the world
culminates the absurd nature of the religion. God is still there,
acknowledged as Creator and Director of the universe. Man, certain that he knows nothing of God's purposes, is left free to
perpetuate in *ice-nine* statuary the response of mankind to life on
earth. Thumbing one's nose at You Know Who involves typical
Bokononist paradoxicalness. The lighthearted grimness of the tone
echoes the undercutting of ending-the-world solemnity by a childish gesture. In the words of Robert Scholes, "What man must
learn is neither scorn nor resignation. . . . but how to take a
joke. . . . Even at the punch-line of the apocalypse, feeble man can
respond with the gesture prescribed by Bokonon, suggesting an
amused, tolerant defiance."[5]

As the author of fictions that allow the illusion of human understanding, Bokonon may seem the benefactor of mankind, but
he himself never forgets that his religion is claptrap and some of
his actions are dubious at best. In his consistent cynicism Bokonon
reveals his kinship with more conventional and exploitative con
men. We learn of certain side benefits to him that come from his
exercise of power. Exiled to the jungle, he none the less regales
himself on the delicacies his faithful followers bring him. The
spiritual leader of thousands, he feels no obligation to take his
own counsel seriously. Thus when several thousand of his surviv-
ing followers capture him and demand an explanation after *ice-
nine* has gripped the world, Bokonon has one set of advice for
them and another for himself. In a note left at the scene of the
crime, an amphitheatre where these thousands have committed
suicide with *ice-nine*, he recounts what happened:

These people made a captive of the spurious holy man named
Bokonon. They brought him here, placed him at their centre,

and demanded him to tell them exactly what God Almighty was up to and what they should do now. The mountebank told them that God was surely trying to kill them, possibly because he was through with them, and that they should have the good manners to die. This, as you can see, they did.   (220)

Bokonon, however, is not so self-righteous that he himself will commit suicide. As he has always maintained, "he would never take his own advice, because he knew it was worthless" (221). Thus Bokonon condemns himself in terms that transfer easily to a more conventional confidence man. The hedonism he proclaims in his religion is violated in principle by this advice because there is no "real" reason for suicide under these circumstances. The conditions of life under *ice-nine* are not unpleasurable. With a massive supply of frozen canned food, available without work in a disease- and pest-free world, these victims might more appropriately live on as long as possible. The one essential lack in their world is a future, but since Bokononism has always presumed the hopelessness of human endeavour, that lack need not justify suicide. Bokonon himself will cynically live on to add to his Books, regardless of the disappearance of the bulk of his followers. They have ultimately served only as toys. He is, after all, a con man.

The first sentence of *The Books of Bokonon* is: "All of the true things I am about to tell you are shameless lies." This paradox and its placing sum up the new explicitness Vonnegut gives to his portrait of the con man. With Bokonon there is no coyness about his lies; from the outset his victim can only be a knowing, even if reluctant, disciple. In this world the only truths must be lies. Bokonon so dominates his fictional world that he becomes virtually indistinguishable from it. Everywhere one turns in *Cat's Cradle*, from the epigraph on, Bokonon has been there before.

Even granting that Bokononism is an ironic and self-deflating sort of religion, Vonnegut brings extraordinary new status to the confidence figure. Given an insane world, Bokonon makes the most sense of it that is possible. Once a con man can found a new religion, become even a bogus Messiah, he has risen higher than ever before in human esteem. His apotheosis emerges in John Fowles' portrait of Maurice Conchis in *The Magus*.

NOTES

1. See Meeter's "Vonnegut's Formal and Moral Otherworldliness", in *The Vonnegut Statement*, edd. Jerome Klinkowitz and John Somer (New York, 1973), 209.
2. All quotations from Vonnegut follow the identical pagination of the hardbound Delacorte edition and the paperbound Delta edition, in the present instance page 162. All further quotations will be identified by page numbers in parentheses.
3. Giannone, however, finds this nicety only in the hardbound Delacorte edition whereas it appears also in my copy of the Delta paperbound. Readers of the Penguin edition, alas, are deprived not only of this mathematical jibe at rationality but also the table of contents itself. See Giannone's *Vonnegut: A Preface to His Novels* (Port Washington, N.Y., 1977), 68.
4. See Tanner's *City of Words: American Fiction 1950–1970* (London, 1971), 191.
5. See Scholes' *The Fabulators* (New York, 1967), 44.

7

John Fowles and the Con Man as God

To do is to act; so all doers are actors.
—Melville, *The Confidence Man*

The Magus (1966) is John Fowles' first novel in order of writing, though the second in order of publication. Through the 1950s as he wrote and rewrote it, the working title was "The Godgame".[1] That identification of the activities of master con man Maurice Conchis and his collaborators signals the contemporary apotheosis of the confidence figure. They earn the label by impressive control over the context in which their victim thinks he lives until the moment when they choose to "disintoxicate" him from the game so that he too can play god in his own right.

The godgame follows the archetypal strategy of a con game. The young Englishman who serves as victim eagerly insists that the game continue once he has tasted a few tidbits. Since his primary greed is not monetary but sexual, the godgamers simply offer bountiful gain in the coin of his realm—the love of his highest fantasy female, his *anima*. By mid-game he is enchanted so thoroughly that he commits his full reserve funds, the one relationship of his life that approaches love. When the con men—and women—decide he is inextricably entangled, they fleece him, leaving him as outraged and cold as a new-shorn lamb in an alpine winter.

This game does not even end there, for Fowles asks his reader to believe that these manipulators, though ruthless in their tactics, are beneficent in their impositions. The mystifications, seductions, and humiliations foisted on the victim claim to open for him the possibility of loving contact with another human being. But in order to love and hence claim his humanity, he must himself become a conscious manipulator, a con man, a magus. The ultimate implications accord with Auden's epigraph to this study: in this day and age good will can only find a "confessedly theatrical" expression.

Even before such paradoxes are tested against the fiction, they startle as a giant step in the progressive legitimizing of the confidence figure that has been emerging through these portraits. Gone is the back-handed and playfully nihilistic justification for Bokonon's falsehoods. A world away lie the early identifications of the con man as a devilish threat to mankind. If Conchis, and behind him Fowles, have their way, the con man will be enshrined as the only benevolent force credible in the kind of post-Christian world they project. They presume a vaguely post-war existentialism which rules out God but not the value of love. Love consists primarily in accepting responsibility for the existence of another, a humanism robbed of sense or justification by the lack of a coherent or comprehensible world. If God is dead, he must be replaced—absurdly—by godgamers who take his vacated responsibilities into their own hands. Their final value will none the less be love. The novel closes with a second-century Latin exhortation from the *Pervergilium Veneris*: "love, whether for the first or the umpteenth time."[2] What is unsettling is that the means for expressing their "love" are indistinguishable from those of the typical con man.

As the con man approaches the *nec plus ultra*, it is once again the victim who recounts the story because only he can serve as a link to the ordinary humanity presumed of the reader. But also the reader is subjected to the godgame of the novelist, the ultimate magus who emerges near the end to share the glory and the paradox of the benevolent manipulator. From the point of view of that novelist, the essential ingredients are three: the victim, a setting in which to play him, and a team of con men. The victim should be young but old enough to feel worldweary and dissatisfied with his life so far. Kill off his parents to create a bit of an independent income; confer on him an Oxford education to suggest a modicum of intelligence and to justify a certain level of cultural allusions. Grant him a flair for empty affairs with women that he can rationalize in terms of a purposeless universe. Call him Nicholas Urfe, twenty-five years old in 1952 when the story opens to his latest affair.

The appropriate setting must be relatively distinct from the victim's usual haunts if the game, as in this case, stretches over several weeks or even months. The con men will be in a stronger position if the setting is sufficiently isolated for them to control mail and other forms of communication. Hence, imagine a little-populated Greek island complete with a boys' school where the victim, in his fitful desire for a change, can have a job teaching English. Call the island Phraxos. Construct a villa in one remote corner and stock it with all the props necessary to the staging of the game, including concealed living quarters for off-duty actors. Call it Bourani and add a private beach for easy boat access and for intimate encounters.

Then the team, the most difficult factor of all. Since sex is the name of the game, conceive a woman capable of playing the succession of roles best suited to entice this particular victim. Add an identical twin for the sake of double-takes. Season with a competing male to arouse jealousy. Serve up supported by servants and other walk-ons sufficient to ensure credible local colour. Explain the motivation of these actors by implying that they themselves, at least the principals, have experienced earlier godgames from the receiving end, an experience which has transformed them into willing collaborators.

Also, since the activities of this group are to be still more intricate than those of Gide's *"mille-pattes"*, their work must be co-ordinated. Conceive, then, a chief orchestrator suitable to the occasion: a mature man who by his obvious wealth and his easy familiarity with the highest of European culture can command the respect of the young victim. Include piercing eyes, authoritative knowledge of diverse scientific fields, mastery of hypnosis and obscure ties to the occult. Give him a Greek origin to make him at home on location, but place his youth in England to open easy contact with the victim. Call him Maurice Conchis, the Magus. His title and the book's can appropriately come from the tarot deck because it suggests the mysterious and intriguing aura useful to involving the victim—and the reader—in the story. In addition Conchis' name, literally "shell" in Greek, is pronounced,

Peter Wolfe reminds us, like "conscious". Two additional associations from modern British slang will also find their echoes in the story: a "conchie" is on the one hand a conscientious objector to war and on the other the operator of a shell game, a county-fair con.[3]

The con man cannot, however, tell his own story without being inevitably suspect, as we have seen in the cases of Felix Krull and Clamence. In this case a detached observer would seem too distant and impersonal, for this is to be the story of a quasi-religious con version, a parable. Therefore the victim makes the best narrator since only to his eyes do events unfold progressively. To the con men, no matter how much they may need to improvise, the broad outlines of the game and its goal are foreseeable. The victim's first-person autobiography, however, must screen out his post-game consciousness, for that would give away too early and easily the unfolding drama of his entrapment. The reader would be cheated of his vicarious replay of victimization. Besides, the narrator's candour gains him credibility as he recounts as if living them the progressive stages of his involvement, painful as it becomes. At most he can be allowed a few neutral remarks about how some of his attitudes had evolved an indefinite number of years later.

The narrative structure within which these elements interact need not become complicated. The focal point of interest is the unfolding of the game itself through the victim's shifting sense of what is going on. But the development of the game needs to be framed by before-and-after shots of the victim in order to dramatize the impact of the game. Hence three sections, the first and third relatively quite short.

Since the essential thrust of this game moves from sex in the direction of love, the two framing panels of the triptych appropriately portray Nicholas' relations with a woman, a pert, sexy, waif-like Australian named Alison Kelly. As she wanders into Nicholas' bedroom at the age of twenty-three, Alison is a "human oxymoron",[4] a "female boy" (24), who is "innocent-corrupt, coarse-fine, an expert novice" (22). She modulates between the skilled self-assurance of a whore and the sloppy self-pity of a reluctant tramp. What Alison lacks in self-control and sense of direction she makes up in her acute perceptions of others. From the start she recognizes Nicholas as an *"affaire-de-peau* type" (23), a label amply justified by his previous sexual conquests and his ensuing conduct with Alison. Because of her usefulness as a touchstone for what happens to Nicholas, she puts in three appearances: one at the beginning, once in the midst of the game, and then at the end as the final test of its impact on him.

In this first appearance Alison serves to demonstrate the ways in which Nicholas is ripe for the godgame. He is restless and ambitious, particularly in his relations with women. His affairs have to be short because he craves fresh challenges only to let his successive partners drop as he does Alison once she is clearly the more loving one. Nicholas is protected from love by impenetrable defences: his self-absorption and his limitless capacity for boredom. Since sex preempts love, he craves more intriguing challenges than easy Alison. The godgame will provide them.

In the autumn, after a two-month affair, Nicholas disengages himself from Alison with practised skill. He takes up a teaching post at the Lord Byron School for Boys on the fictional island of Phraxos. The winter he spends there in loneliness whets his appetite for excitement. By Easter time boredom and isolation drive him to explore the uninhabited thirty square miles of his island. By late May he has discovered the villa at Bourani, the stage on which he will more than fulfil his desire to be the centre of attention.

There presides Maurice Conchis, master of extraordinary ceremonies, the Magus himself. Conchis commands Nicholas' respect and attention with his piercing eyes and mask-like sixty-year-old face—all told, an intriguing figure to find camped in a lonely villa surrounded by fabulous art works, a massive library which excludes all fiction, and a startling variety of objects with pornographic decorations. The mysterious aura enveloping Conchis expands into the multilayered mysteries of the godgame itself.

The godgame is one of the most elaborate of all stories of con men at work. Here the fleecing of a single victim, deftly unfolded through successive strata of complexity, develops over four hundred-odd pages. Fowles is clearly having a field day of the imagination with results which are almost baroque in complexity. For this *tour-de-force* Nicholas' intelligence is crucial. It allows him to take note of nuances in the show, to associate details that otherwise might remain disconnected, and to generate diverse hypotheses in the attempt to comprehend what is happening to him. The game, like those of all skilled con artists, is so tailored to his personality, his loneliness, his habitual substitution of sex for love, that he would need superhuman defences to escape.

To analyse the shaping of the godgame particular to Nicholas Urfe, I need to distinguish the substance of the game from its method. The game is ostensibly designed to allow Conchis to recount to Nicholas his life story over successive weekends. Through these reminiscences Nicholas and the reader are subjected in retrospect to the major events of European history in this century, particularly the two World Wars. The Conchis story falls conveniently into four stages defined by the nature of Nicholas' involvement. The method of the godgame is at least as important as its formal substance because it draws the victim further and further into the game. By the coda, after Nicholas' distintoxication, method and substance have merged to produce the final impact on his life.

The method is a kind of meta-theatre which works essentially like the process of a Jungian psychoanalysis. In the 1977 revised version of the novel Fowles makes the Jungian background explicit by suggesting it as part of Conchis' psychiatric training. If Nicholas simply heard the Conchis story, he would tend to respond to it as abstract ideas rather than experiencing it in his own emotions. For Jung, this was the greatest danger in any psychological investigation whether in myth research or in direct analysis. Thus the godgamers, for example, expose Nicholas to sensory bombardment which recreates key moments in the Conchis story, for example, the stench of a rotting German corpse in 1917 which turned Conchis forever against war. Still more important, since their crucial target is his innermost emotional self, they expose him, fleetingly at first, to a woman who seems to embody his most cherished fantasy of womanhood, what Jung called his *anima*. The *anima* is deeply buried in the psyche as Jung conceives it. An immature male typically uses it as his ultimate frame of reference for anything to do with the opposite sex, in Nicholas' case as the basis for finding Alison and all the other women in his life unsatisfactory. His profound self-love can be reached by decking out a woman who appears to live out this most cherished of his images. No wonder she seems like a goddess. And no wonder he can be led around by the nose as soon as his *anima* circuits are properly engaged.

In this first stage of the game, Conchis introduces the young woman in question as if she were a projection of his own *anima*. Conchis describes himself at the start of World War I as a young man about twenty who was deeply in love with a Miss Lily Montgomery, a paragon of young English womanhood of the era. After her death of typhus during the War, Conchis, it seems, has never married but instead dedicated his house to her memory. The mysterious young woman appears fleetingly but always in the context of recreating the original Lily in dress, speech, and mannerisms. Despite her obvious physical reality and attractiveness, Nicholas admires most of all her delicate Edwardian femininity.[5]

In this first stage of the godgame the *anima* dimension remains muted. Conchis concentrates on creating an encounter for Nicholas which can simulate the feelings of the battlefield in 1915. Bringing several old teeth, Conchis demonstrates how one contains hydrocyanic acid. He and Nicholas are to play a mock war in a matter of seconds. Nicholas is to roll a die and if it comes up a six, he is to chew one of the teeth. Bullied and shamed into accepting the wager, Nicholas rolls—a six. The die, like war, is fixed; it can roll only sixes. Nicholas, through his horror losing the bet and his shame at backing out of the wager, has been obliged to feel something of the experience of a world "without the possibility of reason" (110).

In the second phase of the game's development Nicholas becomes more conscious of a planned structure, though he does not succeed in defining its purpose. Conchis' narrative and the accompanying dramatic illustrations have a rehearsed air; everything seems to happen on cue. On the other hand, the dramatic sequences do not always illustrate Conchis' experience. "Lily Montgomery" vanishes from the supper table because her brother Apollo has come. Moments later she seems to appear as Diana, the virgin huntress, whose arrow kills a naked man who is pursuing her. Carefully orchestrated stage lighting against the background of the Bourani trees guarantees that all has been carefully planned—but to what end? Conchis offers an indirect explanation by setting Nicholas to read about eighteenth-century French masques, which also included such veiled sexual scenes as Nicholas has witnessed.

118

More evidence of staging appears in Conchis' recounting of his relationship with a Count Alphonse de Deukans, a French aristocrat, dilettante, and collector worthy of the *ancien régime*. Nicholas becomes suspicious when he learns that Conchis was twenty-five when he became de Deukans' *protégé*. The parallel de Deukans-Conchis matches Conchis-Nicholas too perfectly, even to the perpetually silent servants preferred by each master. De Deukans' collecting urge encompassses, like that of Conchis, harpsichords and salacious *objets d'art*. The significance of these parallels eludes Nicholas. He is left to contemplate the cryptic principle de Deukans willed to Conchis along with his fabulous wealth: *"Utram bibis? Aquam an undam?* Which are you drinking? The water or the wave?" (171).

This question is a metaphor just as the notion of a masque is another metaphor for the godgame, but it has special implications for Nicholas' continuing experience. When wave is opposed to water, a distinction is asserted between form and substance. This distinction recurs in later episodes until it becomes clear that Nicholas has encountered a series of waves without substance which vanished each time he took them as "real" and reached out to drink.

The drink ever more tantalizingly offered to Nicholas at this stage of the game is *anima* as "Lily". She continues to play the beauty of 1915 but gives him enough glances and gestures out of character to intrigue him with the possibility of an extra-theatrical relationship with her. Without warning Conchis erases the wave called "Lily" in favour of a new identity for the girl as "Julie Holmes", a schizophrenic with paranoid tendencies whom Conchis is saving from life in an institution. The game is to amuse her in the manner of hide-and-seek, though the seeker must realize that it would be dangerous to become emotionally involved and to trust the tales that "Julie" may recount. This warning is carefully timed to fall on deaf ears. As in all con games, the victim demonstrates that he wants to continue. Nicholas recognizes himself to be hopelessly bewitched by the events at Bourani and above all the elusive feminine creature who has captivated him. Thus he is ready for a test of his loyalties in the form of an interlude between the second and the still more serious third stage of his involvement, an interlude provided by Alison's visit to Athens for a long weekend.

Up to this point in Nicholas' fascination with the mysterious goings-on, the thought of Alison has helped him keep a sense of balance and perspective about the unearthly and stagy scenes that characterize the game. Now he is to meet her in the flesh, though he tries to keep sex out of their meetings. Because Alison has not changed from her warm earthy self, she points up how much Nicholas has evolved under the impact of the godgame. Nicholas finds himself acting toward Alison as Conchis had acted toward him. He relishes his sense of dramatic irony when he plans out how he will present the lie of his having syphilis. He begins speaking about his own early life and his parents with a detached and penetrating ease modelled after that of Conchis. This assimilation of Nicholas to Conchis further dramatizes the latter's power, already implicit in his having hypnotized Nicholas at the close of the second stage.

Alison offers to leave her job and join him on Phraxos, but he refuses, unwilling to give up the multiple promises the game seems to hold. Thus spurned, Alison must reject him completely. All his hopes will rest with the godgame. In criminal con man's slang, Nicholas has been "put on the send", that is, he has gone to deplete his bank account in order to risk all his reserves for the fabulous gains promised by the game at hand. And Nicholas will fare little better in this investment than the victims of con men who are interested only in money.

Once this interlude assures Nicholas' irretrievable commitment to the godgame, the third stage can begin with increasingly serious overtones. Instead of simply following Conchis' recital of events, the dramatic poses and interludes begin to precede the explanation. The game is enveloping Nicholas more and more completely. Concurrently the didactic rehearsal of Conchis' life and Nicholas' *anima* involvement begin to work more closely together. Conchis shows Nicholas how to fish for an octopus with a white rag and recounts his encounter in Northern Norway with a madman who believes he sees God. The moral is the same in both cases. All creatures prefer the ideal to the real; what one thinks one lives is what one lives. With such *exempla* Conchis encourages Nicholas to follow his *anima* fantasies about "Lily-Julie" while she is inflaming him with furtive kisses.

Nicholas is so thoroughly hooked that the godgamers can now

120

play him at will, reshaping the scenario so that he seems ever closer to possessing his *anima*. They wipe away schizophrenia as an explanation for the presence of "Lily-Julie". Now Nicholas is to see her as an actress hired by Conchis for an obscure "experiment in mystification". She claims to have fallen in love with Nicholas and wants him to help her and her twin sister to escape from Conchis. Nicholas is delighted to accept this new version because he can act the liberating crusader who will free the beauteous damsel from the ogre and in the process possess his *anima*. The girls carefully draw him into direct participation in the pretenses; he too must begin consciously acting a role.

Nicholas freely, even eagerly, assents to this new twist in the game though in a more profound sense he cannot choose *freely* because he is compulsively hooked on his *anima*. Before setting him free to create his own scripts, the godgamers want him to perceive the essence of freedom as it emerges in the climactic incident from Conchis' life. This is the didactic core of the third stage of the godgame. As mayor of Phraxos during the Nazi occupation, Conchis finds himself in an impossible situation with only seconds to make up his mind. Three partisans, all horribly tortured, are tied waiting for him to kill them by clubbing. If he fails to do so, eighty hostages from the village will be shot. Faced with this inhuman choice, Conchis is jolted to a new awareness when the head partisan mouths the word *eleutheria*, for freedom is the word which reveals the inner significance of the Nazi experience, which is "the only European experience" (377). By over-riding and demolishing the restraints that held European civilization together, the Nazis made everything possible; freedom was and remains absolute. An individual, in particular Conchis, assumes his full humanity when he accepts the responsibility for *not* performing hurtful actions even though they are permitted, in *not* striking even when all the means and justifications are ready at hand.

Once the moral punch line has been delivered, the game seems to dissolve as it moves into its fourth stage. Nicholas seems to have the upper hand in the contest over "Lily-Julie". Conchis offers a "final" explanation for the game as a kind of improvisational game theatre in which there exist only a fixed point of departure and a fixed conclusion (345). The motivation for the game seems to be escape from boredom for both director and actors.

121

Conchis packs up the props, introduces the actors, abandons the site. All is building nicely toward the consummation of Nicholas' desire for his *anima* figure. But just as she teases him to a frenzy sexually, Fowles is teasing his reader with expectations of a burning "sex scene".[6] Just a moment before possession, Conchis re-enters to overpower naked Nicholas and cart him off drugged to endure the final stage—the disintoxication.

The disengagement of Nicholas from the *anima* figure is emotionally proportional to the intensity of his psychic involvement. Since he has been overwhelmingly committed to the pursuit of his beloved fantasy woman, the pain and humiliation of disengagement are barely tolerable. Nicholas is made to suffer assaults on his inner being that are worthy equivalents for the Nazis tactics Conchis once suffered. And the godgamers continue to act like psychotherapists with a Jungian background. New revelations of the "real" nature of the godgamers succeed each other rapidly. The archetypal emerges explicitly when twelve judges dressed in outlandish costumes file into an Inquisition Star Chamber where Nicholas is tied and gagged on a throne. The figures are redolent with witchcraft, alchemy, mythology, primitive animism, as if to imply that the godgamers are to be understood as manifestations of the collective unconscious so dear to Jung. But moments later the twelve disrobe and claim to be a distinguished international team of psychiatrists who are assembled to deliver to a group of "students" a definitive analysis of Nicholas' personality. They are well enough informed about his past and accurate enough, despite all their jargon, to make Nicholas wince. He feels stripped of any privacy by these demons, particularly his erstwhile *anima*, "Lily-Julie", now coldly dissecting his innards. They even accuse him of masochistic tendencies sufficient to allow him a perverse pleasure in their denigrations.

Suddenly the roles reverse. In the name of justice Nicholas is to be allowed to punish one of their number as a scapegoat for their impositions on him. The proffered sacrifice is, predictably, "Lily-Julie", who is stripped to the waist and tied to a flogging frame. The available instrument is a cat-o'-nine-tails worthy of the British navy two centuries ago. The only limitation is ten strokes and the knowledge that permanent disfigurement would follow excruciating pain. As Nicholas stands with cat in hand and realizes that he is genuinely free to strike, he suddenly relives Conchis' position between the Nazis and the tortured partisans. *Eleutheria* once again, this time experienced. Nicholas, despite all he has endured, accepts his own human freedom not to strike. It is the dramatic climax of the game, though not its final twist.

Now tied himself to the flogging frame, Nicholas must watch a crude pornographic film featuring "Lily-Julie" and her black American bodyguard, Joe. The film even includes clips of love-making taken during Alison's visit to Athens—that privacy too has been raped. At the crucial moment the film runs out to be completed in the flesh by Lily and Joe, the black actor, enacting livingly not only the intercourse Nicholas has longed for in expectant fantasy, but also *Othello*. Thus Lily leaves his life as Desdemona, another role no more revealing of her "true" self than any of those that have preceded it. There is nothing left of either the fantasy or the game, only a final visit from Conchis, who coolly informs the bound and gagged Nicholas that he is now, like them, "elect". He is left to straggle back to the school and pick up whatever pieces of his life he can. Reality, in the godgame, has proved an infinite and empty regress.

These con men are kinder than their criminal counterparts, because they allow Nicholas a chance to recoup his losses, to see the game as a necessary purgation, a bad dream with potentially fruitful consequences. They had led him to believe that Alison was dead, a suicide after his rejection of her. They sent him letters and newspaper clippings which must have been forgeries in the best tradition of criminal con men because a fleeting glimpse of Alison in Athens while he is *en route* for London exposes yet another layer of trickery. They have toyed with his inner life without limit. Yet despite his rage that Alison should have co-operated with them, he soon realizes that she is the one stable entity possible in his life. He must locate her and love her.

Hence the coda, the final section through which Nicholas searches England, tracing down all the clues he can think of, even locating one member of the team. He learns that he must convince Alison that he is able to pay for her after his earlier refusal of her love. His longing is annealed through months of search and waiting. Feeling no longer English but European, he is finally ready in spirit when she appears, ostensibly to inform him that she is returning to Australia. As they walk awkwardly together through Regent's Park, where Conchis and his Lily walked at a pivotal moment in their lives some forty years earlier, Nicholas finds the inspiration he needs to win Alison back. He constructs an instant version of the godgame in which she too must choose out of her own freedom. Thus Nicholas completes the process of imitating Conchis. The trials of the godgame have toughened him into a small-scale magus and con man.[7]

In this way Fowles offers the victim rebirth—if he is able to assimilate the game as a model for his own activities. His mistakes, his greed, his self-absorption can be forgiven. Alison is not dead; Lily was a fantasy woman. There is still a life outside the domain of the game, but the means of redemption are to subject that life to the principles of the godgame.

This final scene rings with echoes of earlier stages in the game. Nicholas proposes the following script: he is to walk away from Alison, she to follow and take his arm, the same repeated a second time, whereupon Nicholas is to deliver a solid slap to the side of her face. The slap echoes a blow given by the Nazi colonel to the chief partisan in the war eposide (323, 570). Alison is then, if she so chooses, to go directly by taxi to Paddington Station, to the waiting room, an echo not simply of Nicholas' several months of waiting for Alison to reappear, but more importantly of the rusted sign that marks the entrance to Bourani: *Salle d'Attente*. Alison is to say nothing about the script, but only to act it or not as she chooses. She has a matter of seconds to decide, as did Conchis facing the Nazi colonel, and Nicholas holding the cat-o'-nine-tails in his hand. *"Eleutheria.* Her turn to know" (569).

Nicholas has now learned that the only access to life-giving water is by *creating* a wave. Both he and Alison in their initial affair played a variety of roles, but without self-awareness and without choice; hence each was victimized by his own and the other's unawareness. After the godgame he (and she, presuming that she chooses to play her part) has learned the necessity of conscious role-playing. Note that the roles encouraged by the god-game are not random but profoundly humanistic. The cardinal commandment is "Thou shalt not commit pain" (556), except of course in the process of helping another victim assume his human-ity, his freedom. Nicholas in particular must also learn to distinguish love from sex, the heart from the loins. Only in such a spirit can a godgame player properly impose his scripts on others.

In the final process of becoming a gamester Nicholas adopts a certain smile that has characterized all the members of Conchis' group. This smile appears first on the battered visage of an ancient Greek sculpture, a smile of "purest metaphysical good humour, a mouth timelessly intelligent and timelessly amused" (132). Conchis and most of his company practice the same expression: a smile suggesting simultaneous attachment and disengagement, a smile of "dramatic irony" (416). The smile is even one touchstone for Conchis' "philosophy": "It is a manifestation of freedom. It is because there is freedom that there is the smile. Only a totally predetermined universe could be without it. In the end it is only by becoming the victim that one escapes the ultimate joke— which is precisely to discover that by constantly slipping away one has slipped away" (375–76). As Nicholas later concludes, "the smile was not so much an attitude to be taken to life as the *nature* of the cruelty of life, a cruelty we cannot even choose to avoid, since it is human existence" (452). Nicholas' right to the smile proceeds not simply from his suffering through the cruelty of the disintoxication, but from his readiness to extend comparable treatment to Alison through the vicious slap he gives her in accordance with his script. It no longer matters whether or not there are members of Conchis' group watching the final action; Nicholas has so internalized the principles of the game that he now perceives his actions to be theatrical in the sense that Conchis has developed.

Conchis' version of game theatre leaves the script fluid in order to invite the creative participation of all the actors, including the unknowing victim. Nicholas, then, has been less a spectator or participant than an unaware actor: " 'Here we are all actors. None of us are as we really are.' He raised his hand quickly. 'Yes, I know. You think you are not acting. Just pretending a little. But you have much to learn about yourself. You are as far from your true self as that Egyptian mask our American friend wears is from his true face' " (345). The moral is clear enough but tangled in paradox. All human life appears minimally theatrical in the sense that individuals are always adopting poses, as we have seen in the initial affair between Nicholas and Alison. Because they did not recognize themselves as actors, they could not be in possession of their "real" selves. But none of the participants in the game are as they *really* are and the game offers no means for defining *real* selves. As Lily coyly remarks, "What is just me?", a multiply elusive remark punctuated by the "Leonardo smile" (410). In the total context of the novel they have no real selves; they are identifiable only by their profound commitment to the game; they are, after all, confidence men and women.

Nicholas in time realizes that Conchis' cohorts are involved from their own deep conviction of the rightness of their procedures. At the climax when Nicholas decides not to use the cat to punish his tormentors, he concludes: "I knew they were only actors and actresses, but that even the best of their profession cannot in silence act certain human qualities, like intelligence, experience, intellectual honesty; and they had their share of that. Nor could they take part in such a scene without more inducement than money; however much money Conchis offered" (440). The amount of money required to mount the godgame is, as Malcolm Bradbury remarks, "great and improbable".[8] The inducement for the actors is ostensibly that they have undergone experience comparable to those Nicholas has endured. They in turn chose to perpetuate and extend the godgame. Lily de Seitas, for example, who was introduced to the game before 1939 appears to Nicholas as "playing a role so deep-rooted in fidelity to concepts I did not understand, to people I did not like, that it had almost ceased to be a role" (516). It had ceased to be simply a role for her because it had become the definition of moral reality, a definition inseparable from the game. Even Nicholas shows signs of willingness to help Conchis in later years when he passes up a chance to spoil the fun for the following year's victim.

The morality implicit in the godgame follows from its projected definition of the real as fictitious. In the context of human lives there is no knowable reality beyond the poses men choose to adopt. Therefore each human accepts responsibility for himself by choosing the roles he is willing to play. The godgame requires constant alertness and masterful improvisation as the player develops his individual role in response to shifting circumstances. Thus he exercises his essential human freedom consciously in the context of a game which is designed to bring others to a compar-

126

able consciousness of their own acting and script-writing. As Auden once put it, the world is divided into the sane who are aware they are acting and the mad who are not.[9] No one is innocent, but only the morally mature players accept conscious responsibility for acting out their lives.

This theme is encapsulated in a brief fable Nicholas discovers at Bourani. It is entitled, "The Prince and the Magician". A young prince, having been told by his father that there were no such things as islands, princesses, or God, is amazed to find all three in a neighbouring kingdom. His father insists that none of these are real, in particular "God" because he was dressed in a magician's outfit. The young man returns to the neighbouring kingdom armed with his father's scepticism and reproaches "God" with being a mere magician. The latter admits being bogus, but insists that the boy's father is equally only a magician, as the father later admits. The response to the son's insistent demands yields the moral of the godgame:

> "I must know the real truth, the truth beyond magic."
> "There is no truth beyond magic," said the King.
> The prince was full of sadness.
> He said, "I will kill myself."
> The King by magic caused death to appear. Death stood in the door and beckoned to the prince. The prince shuddered. He remembered the beautiful but unreal islands and the unreal but beautiful princesses.
> "Very well," he said. "I can bear it."
> "You see, my son," said the King, "you too now begin to be a magician." (472)

Whence the godgame. The elect are those who recognize that the real consists only of pretence and proceed so to assault their victims that they too reach the same conclusion and choose to join the troupe, in spirit if not in fact.

By implication Fowles also extends the principle of the game to the conception of the novelist as the ultimate magus. Like a series of nested Chinese boxes the relationship between magus and victim is reiterated on several levels. Nicholas in the end acts the magus toward Alison, as Conchis has already acted the part toward Nicholas. Conchis himself has purportedly learned from his life experience, most particularly from his master de Deukans.

127

Above it all and controlling all is the novelist himself for whom the reader serves as victim and potential convert.

Nicholas begins to define the role of the all-powerful novelist in his attempts to pin down the structure of the game, which appears progressively more akin to the nature of fiction itself. By mid-way Nicholas begins to see Conchis as "a sort of novelist sans novel, creating with people, not words" (214–15). Once he has been disintoxicated, he returns to a similar metaphor.

> All my life I had tried to turn life into fiction, to hold reality away; always I had acted as if a third person was watching and listening and giving me marks for good or bad behaviour—a god like a novelist, to whom I turned, like a character with the power to please, the sensitivity to feel slighted, the ability to adapt himself to whatever he believed the novelist-god wanted. This leach-like variation of the super-ego I had created myself, fostered myself, and because of it I had always been incapable of acting freely. It was not my defence; but my despot.   (460)

Here Nicholas is still somewhat confused and self-pitying because he believes Alison to be dead, but he is clearing the way for a declaration of independence from that internal novelist-superego whom he has tried to satisfy for so long. His freedom will lie in writing his own script and inviting a still less enlightened character, Alison, to join his game.

These references to the magus-novelist-god who actually controls the totality of this fiction prepare the way for his explicit entry. In defence of his implicitly hopeful conclusion Fowles sets out to cry down objections he foresees:

> The smallest hope, a bare continuing to exist, is enough for the anti-hero's future; leave him, says our age, leave him where mankind is in its history, at a crossroads, in a dilemma, with all to lose and only more of the same to win; let him survive, but give him no direction, no reward; because we too are waiting, in our solitary rooms where the telephone never rings, waiting for this girl, this truth, this crystal of humanity, this reality lost through imagination, to return; and to say she returns is a lie.

The notion that Nicholas might recover his girl, have a chance to begin again, may seem hopelessly incredible to contemporary readers who condemn "happy endings" as foolishly sentimental.

Yet this fiction will make capital of its fictitiousness. The girl was lost by the exercise of one kind of imagination when Nicholas rejected Alison for the apparent fulfilment of his *anima* fantasies in the person of Lily. Alison can perhaps be rewon by another form of imagination working through a godgame. Probabilities hardly matter in a world, whether fictional or not, where there are no accepted realities beyond the roles one chooses to play. Nicholas has already received the answer when he inquired about the truth of the incidents of Conchis' life story. If it matters to him whether or not they *really happened*, it would be unkind to answer his question (543). Only when one is beyond posing questions that presume the existence of truth to a humanly graspable reality is one ready to understand the godgame or the fiction which contains it.[10] Fowles' 1977 revised version mutes such explicitness but does not modify the implications of the original ending. Instead of consciously projecting a script which requires Alison's explicit moment of *eleutheria*, Nicholas articulates two stages of script consciousness: first that Alison and he are to understand that the godgamers are watching through the eyes of the classical statues atop Cumberland Terrace, and second, that there is no audience but themselves and their own newly won sense of the theatricality of existence.

In the last analysis *The Magus* in both versions is a parable dramatizing the life-giving function of fiction, fiction as indistinguishable from the techniques of a confidence man. Since nothing beyond the game can be established as real, art has the precious virtue of establishing a context within which roles can make at least temporary sense. As John Fowles puts it in his philosophical tract, *The Aristos*: "Absolute reality is chaos and anarchy, from our relative human standpoint; and our poets are our ultimate corps of defence."[11] In the absence of a supernatural deity, the writer defends us from chaos by the fictions he shapes to offer us a framework in which to choose to live. He becomes a human god, a magus, and also a confidence man of a startlingly benevolent sort. If the magus had set out to plunder mankind, he would have appeared merely devilish as did his counterparts three centuries earlier. Of course, the confidence-man-god remains free, as do other men, to choose the roles he will play; his freedom permits all. In this case he chooses to use his power of pretence not simply to bring his victims under his control but ultimately to enlighten them, to lead them to a conscious acceptance of their own inherent condition of confidence-man-hood. In the absence of God mere humans rise to the godgame.

NOTES

1. See James Campbell, "An Interview with John Fowles", *Contemporary Literature*, 17 (Autumn 1976), 458.
2. I am grateful to my colleague Professor François Paschoud for this reference, which I translate freely. Fowles confirms this source in his foreword to the revised edition of *The Magus* (London, 1977), 7.
3. See Peter Wolfe, *John Fowles, Magus and Moralist* (Lewisburg, Pa., 1976), 103. For the slang resonances I am grateful to my colleague Professor George Steiner.
4. *The Magus* (London, 1968), 19. All succeeding references to this text are identified by page numbers in parentheses.
5. In circumstances under which the *anima* can be found in real life, it is typical that she should follow the models of femininity associated with an earlier generation. James Morris, who thanks to a sex change could literally become his *anima* as Jan Morris, embodies a femininity idealized from several decades earlier. See *Conundrum* (London, 1974).
6. In the 1977 revision Fowles supplies the sexual consummation. While his revisions in almost all instances tighten the style and the con game, this modification is questionable. In the original Nicholas remains sexually frustrated and hence receives the full punch of the disintoxication when black Joe copulates with "Lily-Julie-*anima*". Once Nicholas has achieved his initial sexual conquest, the emphasis shifts toward his hopes for future continuation. Since the reader is asked to believe that sexual fulfilment has in no way dimmed Nicholas' *anima* fantasies, he is asked to extend his respect for "Lily-Julie's" acting ability to superhuman heights. In short the possibility of a "real" attraction and consummation between Nicholas and his *anima* clashes with the moral implications of the godgame. See, in particular, revised version, pages 487 and 627.
7. Robert Scholes confirms this interpretation in "The Orgastic Fiction of John Fowles", *The Hollins Critic*, 6 (December 1969), 7. This article is especially important since Fowles has described it as what he himself would write. See above, note 1.
8. *Possibilities: Essays on the State of the Novel* (London, 1975), 265.
9. *The Age of Anxiety* (New York, 1947), 109.
10. Thus we find once again the recurrent dismissal of "reality" in relation to a con man's fiction. Internal consistency must suffice for victim and reader in Mann, Camus, and Vonnegut as well.
11. Revised edition (London, 1968), 210.

8

Conclusions: The Future of the Con Man in Literature

The Magus completes the cycle of moral revaluation of the confidence figure that has emerged through these portraits. The con man as devil has come in from the cold to be enthroned as an epitome of admirable human types. In the process traditional Western values are stood on their collective heads. In particular there disappears the moral significance of congruence between inner self and outer presentation of self—the sincerity so dear to the Romantics, or the authenticity praised by some of their twentieth-century offspring. Of course, the undermining of sincerity as a value has been explicitly underway for more than a century now quite independently of reference to the confidence figure. Nietzsche, Wilde, and Yeats among many others wrote in praise of masks. As the late Lionel Trilling points out, even Emerson caught a glimpse of what was to come when he noted in his journal for 1840: "There is no deeper dissembler than the sincerest man."[1]

As this study indicates, however, Trilling is simply wrong when he says that "the hypocrite-villain, the conscious dissembler, has become marginal, even alien, to the modern imagination of the moral life."[2] The confidence characters studied here demonstrate how this character type incorporates the mainstream displacements in modern moral conceptions. If, as Auden's epigraph suggests, we in this age are suspicious of those who lay claim to our confidence via an "honest, manly style", the characters studied here exemplify step-by-step the arrival of such a perspective, a process more easily perceived when a single character type can serve as touchstone.

If a certain slippage between inner and outer person comes to seem natural if not inescapable in humankind, the con man triumphs as a specialist in lubricants. No traditional selfhood or integrity survives his slipperiness. He wilfully masquerades in any identity likely to elicit the confidence of those who naïvely presume a direct connection between human appearances and realities. As the con man rises in status through these works, fakery appears more inevitable and less reprehensible. Also the con man's defining characteristic, in literature as in criminal life, that of exacting moral complicity of his victims, guarantees that the reader as well as the victim must cope with awareness of slippage.

The process of upward revaluation of the con man incorporates a radical change in the value placed on consciousness. For Milton sin consisted of eating the fruit of the Tree of Knowledge; insofar as there is something like sin for the later writers in this study, it is associated with remaining unconscious of the grounds of one's being. Melville, Gide, and Mann provide the intermediate steps. In Melville consciousness is blocked by an epistemological impasse, though the author implies that he would be ready to apply a traditional bi-polar morality based on good and evil if only he could clearly identify con men at work. Gide undercuts bi-polar judgments by collapsing all men, in particular the apparently respectable, into the hypocritical and the criminal. His aim is not to reaffirm traditional values but to clear the way for a new amoral aesthetic consciousness. Mann takes a complementary but opposite tack: instead of reducing the respectable to the status of the con man, he raises the latter to the conventionally acceptable status of the bourgeois.

The last three works in this study form a tighter sequence. They invite chapter titles with religious overtones because they proffer progressively grander forms of "salvation" based on consciousness of manipulation as central value. For Camus' Clamence "sin" is the attempt to avoid moral self-condemnation. He who follows Clamence into awareness of his true moral situation must become a self-condemning judge whose authority derives from his superior consciousness and candour. In Vonnegut the equivalent of sin is rather the stupidity of trying to maintain that the world can make sense or be improved. The narrator finds himself obliged

132

to abandon his Christian and liberal humanistic values in favour of the wacky and bogus religion of Bokonon, thereby embracing a "higher" consciousness. In *The Magus* the comparable virtue lies in Nicholas abandoning his early unconscious role-playing, which yields only human hurt, in favour of the conscious manipulation practiced by Conchis and the god-gamers. Wilful pretence, which once appeared evil, has become a moral necessity.

The portraits which engineer this transvaluation of the con man embody a parallel progression in literary form. I am not thinking here of the episodic plot, the setting which guarantees anonymity, or the plurality of victims endemic to the con man. These remain relatively stable concomitants of literary settings of the figure. More sensitive to the issue of moral status is the relation the author establishes between the reader and the confidence figure. Melville, for example, begins where Greene and Milton left off, associating the reader with an observer who is ostensibly disengaged from both con man and putative victims. Melville's reader relates to the fictional events as would a judge at a trial, except that neither he nor the narrator can be sure who is guilty of what. Gide's reader still sides with a formally detached observer-narrator, but he is taken behind the scenes of a con game so that he can see its inner workings. As the epistemological uncertainties disappear, the con man seems no worse than ordinary hypocritical humanity. Thomas Mann carries his reader squarely into the con man's camp by having Felix Krull articulate his own claim to bourgeois acceptance. Mann grants him the narrative status of an equal speaking to equals.

As the con man continues to rise in status, the reader becomes progressively assimilated to the subordinate status of the victim. True, Camus has Clamence tell his own story as did Felix Krull, but the monologue form effectively reduces the distance between unspeaking victim and reader to virtual zero. In Vonnegut the reader's engagement with the con man is through one of the prophet Bokonon's converts. The very reluctance of the narrator to accept the bogus religion affirms to the reader the final compellingness of Bokononism. Finally, John Fowles exalts magushood by focusing the reader's attention through a victim who in the long run becomes an independent practitioner of the confidence arts. The literary impact of the progression is inescapable: as the confidence figure gains in status, the reader's point of engagement with his story becomes progressively more subordinate to him.

As the reader is situated progressively closer to and then subject to the confidence figure, the controlling mechanism (see also discussion above, pp. 99–100) is point of view, but under no circumstances can the reader feel he is getting closer to the "real" confidence man. As we saw at the beginning of this study, a con man properly speaking has no self that is distinguishable from the postures he adopts for his victims. Hence no narrative posture can reveal him off stage and out of costume. Even when the con man tells his own story, as in Mann and Camus, retrospective narration of events combines with confession of manipulation in the present retelling to keep the reader uncertain of the truth-value of the whole. When the victim narrates the tale, as in Vonnegut and Fowles, he once again does so retrospectively, because the victim can only recognize himself as such after he has been taken. If he once recognized a con man at work before that point, he could disengage himself before the fleecing—in literature just as much as in criminal life.

In literature the con man is associated as easily with the artist as with the criminal. After all, he generates fictions for his victims while himself inhabiting a fiction generated by the writer for his readers. Hence the con man as central character automatically reflects his creator's conception of authorship and his sense of the role of the fictive in human existence. On the one hand, these portraits record a philosophical and moral evolution implicit in our growing sense of the centrality of fictions in our lives. On the other, they embody the conception of fiction affirmed by their authors. What is at stake here is the relation of these particular works to the broad evolution of fiction as a medium over the last century or so, in short, the relative "modernity" of the fictional vehicles which contain these confidence figures. In this perspective our authors do not succeed one another in chronological order.

To establish the terms of discourse here, a bit of theory is necessary. A fiction exists thanks to an implicit contract between author and reader whereby the latter promises to give temporary credence to an imitation world in return for entertainment and/or enlightenment. Occasionally an author will share a sense of superior

134

sophistication with his reader by throwing in a character who foolishly forgets the terms of the contract which has brought the two together. Thus in Faulkner's novelette "The Old Man" we see his protagonist going to prison because he attempted to carry out in real life a mail-train robbery he read about in a piece of cheap detective fiction. The catch, of course, is that "real life" in this context is the fictional life to which Faulkner has invited his reader to give temporary credence.

This shared duplicity between author and reader has received numerous and time-honoured justifications. Its importance here is to establish the conventional case in fiction. Most of the novels treated in this study fall to one degree or another under such conventional contracts. The initial lie shared by writer and reader establishes the fictional reality within which a confidence man appears to carry on his characteristic shenanigans by adopting one or more fictitious personae for the sake of his fellow characters. He is recognizably a con man when his habit of adopting false identities contrasts with the more stable identities of other characters. All this is clear enough, though the grounds for future complexities are already present. As a maker of fictitious identities residing within a fiction, the confidence man embodies his creator's conception of fictivity.

In relation to these criteria the works studied here embody diverse degrees of fictitiousness. The most recent work, Fowles' *The Magus*, is in fact the most traditional in fictional conception and hence narrative strategy. Nicholas d'Urfe is an earnest narrator whose seriousness of tone and solidity of description offer the reader grounds for confidence in the (fictional) reality of the events described. The extravagant pretences of the godgame are to be taken as the "real" experience of the narrator. Although Mann's Felix Krull also lays claim to the trust of his reader by the detailed recounting of his experience, he begins to shift the terms of the contract when he admits to tampering with the "truth" for the purpose of story-telling. Camus in *The Fall* pushes the issue further when Clamence not only admits that he may be inventing his life story out of whole cloth, but goes on to identify his confessing of manipulatory method as necessary to conning his victim. Once the narrator has demolished any trustworthy relation between his confession and the "real" world, the listener-reader must accept the responsibility if he submits to Clamence. Vonnegut and Gide go noticeably further in detaching their fictions from the conventional contracts of realistic fiction. Gide uses the romantic irony and self-mockery of the *sotie* to undercut the seriousness of both traditional morality and conventional fiction. In *Cat's Cradle* the choppy narration, banal parodies, and off-key cultural allusions help undercut the possibility of a reader taking the world of the fiction too seriously.

But of all these works, the most "modern", the most radical in terms of traditional fictional contracts is Melville's *The Confidence Man*. The entire universe emerges as fiction created by the Author of authors. Melville's fiction is, point for indeterminate point, a model of all existence. Reality has become indistinguishable from fiction; no referents are sufficiently unequivocal to serve as a basis on which the reader could confidently identify con men at work. The conventional relationship between con man and victim has been transferred to the relationship between author and reader. Pretence and fakery appropriate to a con man seem perversely to control the unfolding of the text. More than one reader has given up in exasperation once he found himself unable to grasp with any clarity what "reality" was being depicted in the narrative.

This type of fiction, to borrow a term from Stanley Fish, is a "self-consuming artifact",[3] that is, a fiction which instead of building its way toward a climax tears down, confuses, or contradicts what it has just built. Instead of the fiction serving as a window opening onto a certain world, it is a troubled glass that calls attention to itself by the scrambled messages it projects. The aim of such a work is less to entertain its reader than to engage him in a reflective questioning of the grounds on which he accepts fictions or indeed any other means of projecting or perceiving shape or meaning in the world. Hence the reader is thrown back to the assumptions on which he presumed to begin reading. At test are the limits of fiction itself, or better, the limits to the fictitiousness of fiction.

Professor Fish develops this notion primarily to deal with seventeenth-century and some earlier literature, a location in cultural time which will require some changes in conception when we come to discuss Melville's version of the self-consuming artifact. But treating Augustine and Donne and George Herbert, among others, has certain advantages that Fish exploits. Their fundamental Christian orientation allows Fish to place their potentially perverse self-cancellations in the Christian tradition of the Good Physician, who must hurt in order to heal. The sermons of Augustine and Donne are ultimately given over to God, whose presence beyond language is the vision to which the literary work wants to convert its reader. Such a work, says Fish, is

> didactic in a special sense; it does not preach the truth, but asks that readers discover the truth for themselves, and this discovery is often made at the expense not only of a reader's opinions and values, but of his self-esteem. (1–2)

The strategy of such works is anti-rational and anti-discursive in that it dissolves distinctions between places and things in "the light of an all-embracing unity" (3). The artifact is self-consuming in two senses: "the reader's self (or at least his inferior self) is consumed as he responds to the medicinal purging of the dialectitian's art, and that art, like other medicines, is consumed in the workings of its own best effects" (3).

Thus far, with one crucial difference, Fish's conception applies rather well to Melville's *The Confidence Man*. It too, as we have seen, proceeds by self-cancelling narration which leaves characters and their motivations, events and their causes ultimately undefined. Melville's style is qualified out of any significant assertiveness or sent spiralling around conveniently circular puns. Melville's reader as well is likely to be driven by frustration out of his habitual stance as a reader, but if he follows Melville's lead and contemplates the grounds of this fiction, he will discover why it is called *The Confidence Man*. This is the essential difference between Fish's seventeenth-century self-consuming artifacts and Melville's —a matter of confidence, or faith if you prefer. The metaphor of the Good Physician no longer holds because Melville can no longer place his confidence in the Christianity which gave it life. His work belongs not to the God who can be believed to exist beyond all human artifacts, including rational knowledge, but to the Confidence Man of whom one can know nothing more certain than that all his actions and words are equivocal.

Melville, then, is in a paradoxical situation. He makes a self-consuming work not as medicine for the sinner but as the literary equivalent for the universe as he has come to not understand it. Everything turns on the placing of confidence, an act for which there is no adequate justification on any level. To label Black Guinea and his friends as con men is to place one's confidence in the black view of life; to place trust in them is optimistic and equally arbitrary. Even the cynic must finally place his trust somewhere and hence the Cosmopolitan, as figure for confidence itself, plays the tune to which all dance—except one Herman Melville as author of *The Confidence Man.* He has placed his trust nowhere, not even in the literary artifact itself. The supposed referent of literature, the "real world", is just as equivocal, as undefinable, as fictitious, as the literary work itself. "God" is simply the name for the ultimate Creator of fictions on all levels in literature and life. He remains an apparent con man on a universal scale because his world leaves humankind, including readers of Melville's masterpiece, without means to penetrate the multiple uncertainties facing them. Something further might come of this masquerade, but who could know?

Thus Melville has not only ballooned the idea of the confidence man to its world-swallowing maximum, but also he has pushed fiction to near its post-modern state. He presides over both the beginning and the ending of this study and provides the epigraphs for chapters along the way. He is as much of our own time as his own. As Robert Alter puts it, "There is something profoundly modern about Melville's ambivalent sense of his vocation, combining great excitement at the idea of what the novel might do with a growing vexation of spirit over the truths it will not yield."[4] It should not be surprising that Melville should have developed strategies for fiction that approximate those of our contemporaries. *Moby Dick* proved to be a masterpiece so profoundly out of tune with the readers of its own time that it has found its appreciative public only since World War I. *The Confidence Man* has become readable only in recent years. Only now, perhaps, can the stature and importance of Melville's achievement emerge.

Melville, of course, maintains more semblance of traditional story surfaces than many contemporary writers, but they share with him the premise of unknowability in the way they shape their fictional worlds. Melville, it seems to me, carries the confidence figure as far as it can go and still remain visible in literature. At least there is sufficient semblance of a story to make the reader aware of the possibility if not the likelihood that con men are being shown in action. If the fiction is given over any further to the principles implicit in the con man, into fictitiousness, he himself would disappear out of sight behind the mechanisms of the fiction: everything inconsistent, changeable, shifting, identity-less. Such is the literary terrain against which a con man becomes unrecognizable.

If, as I think, there are limits to the fictitiousness of a fiction in which a confidence figure can appear as such and if contemporary literature is moving steadily in that direction, what in the name of futurology can be the fate of such characters? First, there is no diminution of interest in confidence characters in relatively conventional popular fiction which does not try to push out its own limits; there the character type remains vigorously alive. In *avant-garde* writing, however, the con man disappears to the extent that the principles he embodies are also those in charge of the fiction in which he might have appeared. The two writers in this study who are still active, Fowles and Vonnegut, have moved in such a direction. Thus Fowles as author intervenes more heavy handedly in *The French Lieutenant's Woman*, leaving the possible presence of a confidence character only one interpretive option among others. Similarly, though a good deal less memorably, Vonnegut obtrudes his authorial presence in *Breakfast of Champions*, arbitrarily disposing of characters and situations within the reader's view. Insofar as the author emerges through a representative of his own person to acknowledge his manipulative control over the fiction, no confidence character can acquire fictional substance. Instead, the writer's self-conscious wrestling with the pretences of the fiction becomes the subject of the work. In such cases the confidence man's spirit of pretence has so invaded contemporary writing that he remains out of sight behind the scene, perhaps quietly paring his fingernails, though who could know.

NOTES

1. *Sincerity and Authenticity* (1972), 119.
2. *Ibid.*, 16.

3. *Self-Consuming Artifacts* (1972).
4. See Alter's *Partial Magic: The Novel as a Self-Conscious Genre* (1975), 137. Alter somewhat vitiates the force of his usually perceptive remarks by misattributing a statement of unknowability to the cosmopolitan rather than the Emersonian philosopher Mark Winsome who makes it. The cosmopolitan as proponent of geniality advocates trust in labels and indeed all appearances. See Alter, p. 129, Melville, p. 216, and above, p. 42.

Index

141